# LOCAL MAN
## (SAD BUT TRUE STORIES)

Publications International, Ltd.

**Contributing writer:** Lisa Brooks

**Cover art:** Shutterstock.com

**Interior art:** Art Explosion, except 166 (Getty) and 243 (Shutterstock.com)

Louis Weber, CEO
Publications International, Ltd.
8140 Lehigh Avenue
Morton Grove, IL 60053

ISBN: 978-1-68022-581-5

Manufactured in Canada.

8 7 6 5 4 3 2 1

# CONTENTS

# INTRODUCTION

Locals know all of the best stories. They know all of the dirt on their neighbors, and they have cousins that have seen things that you'll never believe. The talk of a small town is mighty and there is no way out once you become the subject of their banter.

*Local Man* is a compilation of strange but verified stories from across the U.S. and even the world, giving us a glimpse into the funny, stupid, reckless, and sometimes brave things locals get themselves into. Sometimes the cops get involved and sometimes it's better that they don't. Sometimes people see things in the forest that scare them and sometimes they see something in their own home. You never know when a local will get into a situation that will become the talk of the town, but you can rest assured that there will always be a new story you haven't heard yet.

There's no stopping locals from getting into the situations they get into, but it's when locals don't think about their actions that the stories seem too strange to be true. Read about reckless or inebriated (or both) drivers, burglars who leave trails of evidence behind them, skeptics who see lights in the night sky, teenagers who take pictures of ghosts, celebrities who could use a geography lesson, consumers who buy more than you can imagine, collectors who find questionable objects fascinating enough to collect, and gourmets who eat metal. *Local Man* has found no end to the list of locals who have gotten themselves into situations that are sometimes embarrassing and shocking but are always funny.

# CHAPTER 1:
# JUST PLAIN STUPID PT. 1

You'd think that there is a common understanding between what is a smart idea and what is a dumb idea, and maybe there is, but people tend to disregard those categories and do what they want anyways. Sometimes you have to do something stupid to make up for mistakes that need to be corrected. Sometimes you have to do something stupid because you don't have a better idea. What types of stupid things would you do if you locked yourself out of your house? Would you call a locksmith, break a window, or try to rappel down to your patio? Well, if you want to get just plain stupid, the correct answer is the last one, obviously.

You might not understand the sound reasoning that takes place before the decision to act is made, but you can clearly understand the end result as stupid. It's often a choice that comes with a whole array of stupid decisions to make, but the stupidest one is usually the simplest way out of a horrible situation, leading to a whole new set of problems to be solved.

People may say stupid things or they may do stupid things, but we don't discriminate between talk and action—it's all stupid. You can never be surprised these days with all of the ridiculous stories found online, ranging in stupidity from celebrities to locals; the playing field has evened out for all of us to act as stupid as we want. Hopefully, as people commit their stupid acts, they don't garner the attention of local police or press, but most of them do.

## CELEBRITIES CONTINUE TO ASTOUND AFTER THE SPOTLIGHT IS GONE

*Celebrities may have held the attention of millions with their stunning performances and public feats, but sometimes they attract more attention to themselves with their airheadedness. Maybe that's a little unfair since a lot of celebrities are constantly bombarded with photographers and reporters. They rarely have time to themselves, let alone some private time to do the stupid things we all tend to do once in awhile. Celebrities can control their image with extreme care and precise self-awareness, but things are bound to slip once in a while.*

*It seems like celebrities who have been in the limelight for a majority of their lives have a little more difficulty hiding their stupidity than the celebrities who were crowned later in life. Maybe it's the lack of attention they paid in school as their dreaming minds focused on their hopes of fame, or maybe it's just a complete lack of awareness of anything outside the scope of the spotlight. Whatever it may be, people caught in the public eye are much more likely to gain the attention of the media by doing something stupid than your ordinary, hard-working citizen, and that's the price they pay for fame.*

## CELEB CLAIMS THAT STORMS ARE CAUSED BY NEGATIVITY

In October 2012, the East Coast of the U.S. was preparing for Hurricane Sandy. The huge storm killed 233 people in the U.S., Canada, and the Caribbean, and caused about $75 billion in damage, becoming the second-costliest hurricane in U.S. history.

As the storm was bearing down on the Atlantic coast, people were scurrying to prepare the best they could. Lindsay Lohan, however, wasn't worried. In fact, she didn't think that anyone else should be worrying, either. She famously Tweeted:

"WHY is everyone in SUCH a panic about hurricane (i'm calling it Sally)..?) Stop projecting negativity! Think positive and pray for peace."

Not only did Lohan not know enough about the hurricane to realize its name was "Sandy" and not "Sally," but apparently she was also under the impression that negativity is the cause of hurricanes.

### RUNNING ON WATER

Reza Baluchi is an ultra-marathoner who has run across the United States twice. But a recent challenge proved to be too daunting, and attracted the ire of the Coast Guard.

Baluchi was attempting to "run" in an inflatable bubble from Florida to Bermuda—a feat he had already tried in 2014. The Coast Guard had to rescue him during the 2014 attempt, when he became disoriented and asked for help. The rescue cost taxpayers $144,000.

When the Coast Guard learned that Baluchi was planning to try again, they sent him a letter ordering him not to depart "because your vessels and the conditions under which you are attempting to complete your voyage to Bermuda is unsafe."

The "vessel" Baluchi was traveling in is called a "HydroPod," and is not unlike a giant inflatable hamster wheel. On his website, Baluchi describes how the temperature within the bubble can reach 120 degrees. "Being inside the HydroPod is not going to be a walk in the park, it will be very hot and humid. One can easily dehydrate quickly and lose breath," he writes.

He had planned to catch fish, eat protein bars, and sleep on a hammock inside the pod. But when the Coast Guard learned that Baluchi was back in the water with his HydroPod, they towed him back to land, stating that "he violated a USCG order not to embark."

Perhaps the ultra-marathoner should stick to running on land.

## CELEB CONFUSED ABOUT HOMETOWN GEOGRAPHY

Actress Raquel Welch was born in Chicago, Illinois. So she should know a few things about it. Like, for instance, the fact that it's a city, not a state. But during one visit to her home city she had this to say about it:

"I was asked to come to Chicago because Chicago is one of our fifty-two states."

So not only is Chicago a state now, but apparently we've added two more states to our country!

## CELEB GETS TO SEE THE WORLD BUT DOESN'T KNOW WHERE SHE IS

Britney Spears is known more for her singing than for her knowledge of geography. Which is probably a good thing, since she's said a few strange things about different parts of the world. For instance, she had this to say about the perks of being famous:

"The cool thing about being famous is traveling. I have always wanted to travel across seas, like to Canada and stuff."

And then there was the time she talked about Japan. Or was it Africa?

"I've never really wanted to go to Japan. Simply because I don't like eating fish. And I know that's very popular out there in Africa."

And finally, here's what Britney had to say when someone asked her if she would ever want to appear on Broadway:

"I would rather start out somewhere small, like London or England."

# THIS ISN'T HOW THAT WAS SUPPOSED TO HAPPEN

*Some things don't go as planned. You might have a perfect plan on how to get your cat out of the tree, but once you get in the tree and grab your cat, it begins to use all four sets of its claws on you as it freaks out. Soon after that, you may realize that your idea wasn't very good at all. The forces of cause and effect can be unpredictable. Who knows how your lover will act when you tell them that you had an affair? You could have the perfect scenario setup to tell them, have all the right words, and the perfect explanation, but you cannot predict whether that hot cup of coffee they're holding will end up being thrown on your face or not. No one can plan for everything, and you can't know what effects will occur in reaction to what you've done, but you can make sure that you lower your risks of being exposed to unintended backfires.*

*Think each of your decisions all the way through. Try to predict all of the positive and negative consequences. Do the consequences add up? Do you think that what you may do will cause a chain reaction of bad situations stemming from this one ill-thought action? If so, it's probably safe to say that you shouldn't do it. Most situations with unintended consequences take their perpetrators by surprise. Decisions done on a whim are very likely to come back and haunt the decider for a good portion of their lives.*

*Here are some things you can almost always avoid to keep yourself from looking like a total fool: Don't shoot your gun at things that aren't an immediate threat to your livelihood. Don't mess with cops, their guns, or their cars.*

*Don't make an agreement with someone that you can't uphold—especially if there is soup involved. Don't hold a position of authority and take advantage of those who are under your umbrella of authority. Don't mess with other people's money. And don't be overly confident. Most of the situations that don't go as planned fall through becasue they weren't thought through. In a situation where you think you don't need to question what you're doing, it's probably a good bet to stop and think about it a little more.*

## CRINGE WORTHY PREDICTIONS COULDN'T BE MORE WRONG

In 1995, astronomer and author Clifford Stoll wrote an article for *Newsweek* magazine about this new thing called the Internet.

Apparently some of Stoll's contemporaries had wild visions for ways the Internet could be used in the future. Crazy ideas like telecommuting, online libraries, and online shopping.

But Stoll wasn't buying it. As he said in the article:

"The truth is no online database will replace your daily newspaper, no CD-ROM can take the place of a competent teacher, and no computer network will change the way government works."

To his credit, Stoll later admitted that he'd been shortsighted, calling his article "cringe worthy."

## REDEYE TO TEXAS

Some people have trouble falling asleep on planes. But that was not the case for an unidentified FedEx Express employee, who reportedly fell asleep in the plane while loading cargo for shipment from Memphis, Tennessee, to Lubbock, Texas. He didn't wake up until mid-flight.

The employee knocked on the door of the flight deck, but was not allowed in due to safety concerns. The pilots told the man to sit in an extra seat for landing. The man was questioned by Lubbock airport police, but was not arrested.

"There was no criminal intent," investigators said, according to reports.

And FedEx spokesman Jim Masilak released a statement saying, "there was never any danger to our employees or cargo," and that FedEx was "fully cooperating with investigating authorities."

## NO SOUP, NO SUBSTITUTION, NO SETTLEMENT

Dwain Downing, an attorney in Arlington, Texas, is suing a diner called Our Place. The infraction? The diner ran out of soup.

Downing had lunch at the diner one Saturday when the restaurant ran out of soup for the $7.95 lunch special. According to Downing, owner Benji Arslanovski refused to discount the price or offer a substitute side.

Instead of simply complaining to the owner, Downing threatened a lawsuit.

In a letter to the owner, in which he misspells the owner's name as "Arslanskobi," Downing demands $2.95—the cost of an additional side at Our Place—plus $250 in legal fees.

"The menu is an offer for a contract by you," the letter states. "I accepted the offer. This action by you and I created a binding contract which is legally enforceable in a court of law."

The diner's weekly lunch special includes an entrée, two sides, cornbread with honey butter, and soup. Upon learning the restaurant was out of soup, Downing says he asked the server if he could substitute another side dish or get a discounted price for his meal.

According to Downing's letter, "She said that you, the owner, refuse to allow any change or discounted price. The onsite manager came over and verified that this was your policy."

Arslanovski told reporters that he'll "take it to court."

"Isn't it amazing?" he added. "This could have been solved with a simple phone call, and he could have come by and gotten a free cup of soup."

Downing's letter demands that the lunch policy at Our Place be changed. But apparently he does recognize that a lawsuit is going a bit overboard.

"It's much ado about nothing," he admits. "But at two in the afternoon, you shouldn't be running out of that special soup."

## BOSS EXPANDS BONUS PACKAGE TO INCLUDE PICK-ME-UPS

Employees always appreciate a bonus for a job well done. It's always nice to have your hard work confirmed and appreciated. Some people like perks on the job, but an auto-body shop in Mankato, Minnesota, was handing out something much different than paychecks.

Jesse Michael Seifert, the owner of Clear Choice Auto Body Repair, was arrested after an employee said that he was handing out methamphetamine for bonuses. Seifert's incentive plan didn't turn out the way he thought it would.

Seifert and his girlfriend, Nancy Jean Loehlein, allegedly handed out a half-gram of meth to each of the shop's six employees.

Agents of the Minnesota River Valley Drug Task Force investigated the shop and also found syringes and a digital scale with traces of the drug.

Seifert had previously been arrested for marijuana possession and drunken driving.

## NOTHING SAYS SOUTH LIKE ARMADILLOS AND GUNS

A man in Georgia accidentally shot his mother-in-law as he attempted to kill an armadillo. Authorities say the bullet ricocheted off the animal's hard shell, hit a fence, traveled through the back door of the mother-in-law's home, and hit the recliner where she was sitting, striking her in the back.

Larry McElroy's mother-in-law, Carol Johnson, suffered non-life-threatening injuries, and was able to walk and talk after the shooting. McElroy was about one hundred yards away from the home when he shot the armadillo, which he managed to kill. But perhaps McElroy will be more apt to leave them alone from now on.

## TOO YOUNG FOR A TATTOO

Terry Hardy, a gymnastics coach at Park High School in Cottage Grove, Minnesota, was placed on administrative leave after he tattooed a fifteen-year-old girl.

Hardy tattooed the girl without her parents' permission, and was cited for two counts of assault. At the time, Minnesota law required written authorization from parents before anyone under eighteen could get a tattoo. The law has since changed, requiring that anyone who gets a tattoo be eighteen years of age, regardless of parental permission.

The girl also received a tongue piercing from Hardy. In an interview, she recalled that halfway through the tattoo, Hardy asked "Is your dad going to be mad?"

"In the middle of a tattoo that's kinda a dumb question," she added.

According to the girl, Hardy told her he has a license to perform tattooing, but he doesn't.

And the girl's dad is none too pleased with the conduct of the coach. "Why is he bringing fifteen-year-old girls to his house?" the father said to reporters. "That's just not right behavior." The father reported his daughter's tattoos to the police.

Hardy's school district released a statement that said:

"Allegations have been made against Park High School Gymnastics Head Coach Terry Hardy. Upon learning of the allegations, he was placed on paid administrative leave by the district. He is on administrative leave pending further investigation as the head coach of Park High School gymnastics, but has been dismissed as a gymnastics coordinator for District 833s community education program."

# STUPID PEOPLE WITH ACCESS TO CARS

*Cars are the best vehicles for stupid people to express themselves with. People who don't like to think love to get into their cars and continue on their thoughtless spree, possibly leading them on a path of destruction. Cars are the preferred escape method for most bank robbers, jewel thieves, and drunks looking to leave their local bar, but they're also a source of fun for millions of people who have nothing better to do.*

*Some people just drive to relax, to clear their minds of the worry of their days, to try to get away from it all. They turn off their minds and go. They hit the open road without a thought in their head, which might be a good way to relax but it's not safe or smart. One should be as alert as possible while they're driving because their car is a two thousand pound machine that can turn into a weapon in less than a split second.*

*People doing stupid things in their cars haven't always done stupid things in their cars. They initially had to pass a test in order to be licensed, but maybe all that information they studied went to the wayside once they felt the thrill of the open road.*

## SUBCONTRACTORS MOVE CAR WITH FORKLIFT

Susan Pellegrino and Tom Nahrwold were shocked when their legally-parked SUV was inexplicably moved by construction workers with a forklift. The workers moved the couple's recently-purchased 2004 Infinity SUV up onto the sidewalk, and a neighbor recorded the whole thing.

The bumper and undercarriage of the vehicle were damaged by the forklift. At first, Pellegrino and Nahrwold were baffled by how their car had been moved. "Well, we didn't know until we walked down South 3rd Street the next day and ran into someone who had this footage," Pellegrino claimed. The video shows a construction worker using a forklift to move the SUV.

The couple showed the video to Two Trees Management, the company responsible for the development project, who, in turn, blamed subcontractor RNC Construction.

"We pride ourselves on being good neighbors and have reprimanded our subcontractor for this unacceptable behavior," Two Trees spokeswoman Nicole Kolinsky claimed. "We have been assured that the subcontractor will fully pay for any damages."

The couple estimated the repairs to the vehicle will cost at least $2,600.

## WOULD-BE DUMB DRIVER CAN'T DRIVE

Many of us who grew up with automatic-transmission cars are thrown for a loop when we encounter a manual transmission. But one would-be car thief in Phoenix, Arizona, got confused when the car she tried to steal was an automatic.

According to police, a man dropped his kids off at a house one evening and left his car running while he went inside. Meanwhile, Jasmine Hernandez hopped into the running car to make a quick getaway. But when the owner heard his car engine revving, he ran outside to find the woman using the levers that work the headlights and windshield wipers, trying to put the car into drive.

Apparently Hernandez didn't realize that many cars have their transmissions located in the center console. The car owner was able to detain her until police arrived.

## WOMAN JOYRIDES IN POLICE CAR

In less than an hour, Kassandra Ellis managed to steal and completely destroy a University of North Dakota police cruiser.

UND Police received reports of a drunk woman wandering around the Hamline Square Apartments, and arrived to the complex in two cruisers. While they were trying to locate the woman, she managed to jump into one of the cars and drive away.

UND Police Sergeant Danny Weigel said, "Officers responded to that area, attempted to locate that person, and were unable to do so. A short time later they left the building and noticed that one of the patrol vehicles had been stolen."

Officers say that after stealing the car, Ellis rolled it into a ditch off Highway 2 near the University of Minnesota Crookston campus.

"It's totaled, there's heavy front-end damage and heavy rear-end damage," Sgt. Weigel said.

Ellis was treated for minor injuries, but may face major penalties for her joyride.

## STUPID LIES CONVINCE STUPID PEOPLE

*Living a lie is a tremendously hard thing to do, especially if you're dumb enough to think you're going to get away with it. It's one thing to tell a lie here and there, but to lie on a consistent basis to the ones you love about the way you live can be a horrible game to keep up with. Each new lie is a new turn on the roadmap of the relationship that must be memorized and followed each time that road is taken again. It's treacherous terrain that is bound to make even the most intricate liar slip up and crash in the ditch.*

*Not only will the fear of being caught continue to add up until one reaches their breaking point, but liars must live with the burden of not being themselves. They wear facades at all times to conceal the truth from others. They sneak around, trying to hide what they really do from others. The life of a liar is filled with worries, stress, and torment that eventually builds up to the moment where they are exposed as what they are: fakes, liars, posers, and fabricators. And when it all comes crashing down, every liar looks stupid for thinking they could get away with what they obviously couldn't get away with.*

## MAN KEEPS HIS JOB AFTER NOT SHOWING UP FOR TWENTY-FOUR YEARS

A man in India last showed up for work in December 1990, but amazingly, he managed to keep his job until January 2015. AK Verma, a senior engineer at the Central Public Works Department, was finally fired after twenty-four years of not showing up to his office. Some see this as a sign that India is cracking down on government bureaucrats who avoid office time.

The newspaper the *Hindu* described Verma as being "on furlough," but in 1992, an inquiry ruled against him. Since then, years of delays and inaction have yielded no results in Verma's situation, and finally, he was fired.

"He went on seeking extension of leave, which was not sanctioned, and defied directions to report to work," officials said in a statement.

According to reports, it is not unusual for civil servants in India to show up late to work, take extra-long lunches, or play golf during work hours.

But work attendance has gone up since Prime Minister Narendra Modi started cracking down on bureaucrats' behavior. He's been known to show up to offices unannounced, and has instituted fingerprint scanners in offices of civil servants. Since the changes, work attendance has gone up, and Delhi's main golf course is mostly empty during the week.

## BURGER KING'S LOW HIRING STANDARDS

Employees of the fast food restaurant in Coon Rapids, Minnesota, received a call one night from someone claiming to be with the fire department. The caller said that the restaurant was pressurized and in danger of exploding, so the employees needed to break all the windows. The amazing part? The employees actually listened and broke multiple windows!

Police are investigating who might have made the prank call.

This isn't the first time a prank caller has targeted a Burger King. In Shawnee, Oklahoma, someone called a Burger King and convinced employees to break windows, claiming there were high levels of carbon monoxide in the restaurant. And a call about a "gas leak" at a Burger King in Morro Bay, California, resulted in $35,000 in damage.

## CHINESE MAN LIVES HIS LIFE AS ONE HUMONGOUS LIE

A man in China, surnamed Yuan, was hospitalized after a car crash. Hospital staff contacted his loved ones, and they began arriving to visit, which at first doesn't seem unusual. But soon, a stream of women between the ages of twenty and forty turned up at Mr. Yuan's bedside. Seventeen women came to visit him in total. None of Yuan's girlfriends knew about the others, and it was only because of the accident that they finally learned of his deception.

Yuan had been dating all the women at the same time. He had a child with one of them, and another was busy planning their wedding. Yuan has now been arrested for fraud in connection with his secret relationships.

"I was really worried when I heard that he was in the hospital," Xiao Li, a girlfriend of eighteen months, told *Xiaoxiang Morning Herald*. "But when I started seeing more and more beautiful girls show up, I couldn't cry any more."

Yuan is accused of regularly taking money from the seventeen women, that he then probably spent on other women.

And his girlfriends weren't the only people that Mr. Yuan deceived. According to *China Daily*, Yuan pretended to have a degree in civil engineering from the respected Central South University, when in actuality he only holds a middle school diploma.

## MEASURING THE RISK

*People can usually stay out of stupid situations if they just take a second to measure the amount of risk they will be taking. People are generally pretty good at that. You can use your reasoning skills to weigh the cost and benefit you might receive from your action. Is it better to take a few side streets to avoid the traffic jam or is it better to wait it out? Should you invest in your little bother's bagel company or not? There are so many instances in the day where you will find yourself asking these questions. You might not even find yourself reasoning between options anymore because it's such a natural process of your thinking.*

*Measuring risk is a human thing to do. You can play the whole scenario out in your head and try to predict how things will turn out, but sometimes things don't go as planned. Sometimes the risks are too large to be avoided, and the imminent repercussions will come crashing down on you. Sometimes trouble is unavoidable, but at least you can find solace knowing that you tried to avoid it the best you could. And then sometimes, you will find yourself wishing you had thought the situation through just a little more.*

## AUSTRALIAN MAN RISKS LIFE INSTEAD OF SPENDING MONEY

Police in Darwin, Australia, rushed to an apartment building in the city after getting reports of a man on the roof. Residents were worried that the man was going to jump. But when police arrived, they found the man with a rope tied around his waist, preparing to rappel down the side of the building to his apartment balcony. He had locked himself out, and apparently had the brilliant idea to climb down the building like Spider Man.

Duty Superintendent Louise Jorgensen said police received a call about a "suspicious male on the roof of an apartment block."

"From all appearances it looked as if he was counting the number of floors down and was preparing to jump," she said. "Police attended and the male was pointed out to them. They rushed to the roof and found the male standing near the edge with a rope attached to a nearby pole."

The police immediately urged the man to move away from the edge of the roof, and asked him what he was doing. That's when the man described his plan to reach his apartment from the balcony, telling police he didn't want to pay for a locksmith.

"But obviously that's a far better option than having to rappel down the building to your apartment," Superintendent Jorgensen said.

## LOCAL PREPARES FOR HIS PHONE TO EXPLODE

A man in Atlanta, Georgia, says he was forced to strip in a Home Depot parking lot because his iPhone caught fire in his pocket.

The embarrassed man, known only as Rocky, says that he was loading his car in the parking lot when he started to feel something burning. Realizing it was his phone, he immediately stripped off his jeans, afraid the iPhone might explode. He later discovered that his phone had been a refurbished model. Apparently, it was also defective.

"When I saw the smoke, I undid my belt, I undid my pants, pushed it away, and turned my head, hoping it wouldn't explode," Rocky says.

The refurbishing company sent him a new phone within twenty-four hours, but Rocky is hoping for "a call from somebody, you know, just taking responsibility for it and apologizing."

### STUPID HIKERS SOON TO BE PUNISHED

You may have heard of Arizona's Stupid Motorist Law, which says that if drivers ignore posted signs and enter flooded areas, they not only run the risk of needing rescue, but they'll also be charged for the rescue. And now, the Phoenix City Council is considering an ordinance for stupid hikers as well.

The idea comes from councilwoman Thelda Williams. She believes that the city should consider banning hiking during periods of excessive heat.

Between January and August 2015, the Phoenix Fire Department responded to about one hundred sixty mountain rescues. The average rescue requires twenty-five people, and if a helicopter is needed, the cost is thousands of dollars per hour.

But while rescues tend to get more publicity when the weather is hot, the fire department says that summer is no busier than any other time of the year. You can go out in the valley at night during any time of the year and watch the helicopters circle Piestewa Peak or Camelback Mountain with their spotlights on.

Nearly every week, people make it to the top of the mountains and then can't get down because it's too dark or they've run out of water. It shouldn't take a crew of twenty-five people and a helicopter every time to save these unprepared hikers.

## REPORTER CLAIMS BACKYARD UNSAFE FOR CHILDREN

Some apparently over-vigilant neighbors reported a Winnipeg, Canada mom to Child and Family Services simply because her children were playing in the backyard.

Jacqui Kendrick is a stay-at-home mom who often allows her three children, ages two, five, and ten, to play in the fenced-in backyard after school. But one day, a CFS worker showed up unexpectedly, saying there'd been a complaint about her children being unsupervised.

Kendrick says she's always either with the children, or watching them from her living room, and the ten-year-old helps to look after the younger siblings.

The questions asked by the CFS worker were upsetting, Kendrick says. "(The worker was) asking me about if we've ever dealt with CFS before, what my childhood was like, how I punish my children. She had to look to see where my kids slept. She had to see if we had enough food in the house."

Kendrick now worries that since a complaint has been filed, any future complaints could result in her children being taken away.

Manitoba's Child and Family Services Act permits a child twelve or older to stay home alone, but says nothing about children playing in a backyard.

## NO HELP IN PUTTING OUT A FIRE

A man from Plantation, Florida, attempted to save his burning home by running down the street to the firehouse to inform the emergency crews that he needed their help. A sixty-seven-year-old man, Neville Morrison, noticed that his house had caught fire and thought quickly of what to do.

Knowing the average response time for firefighters to respond to a call would take too long, he ran barefoot down the street to the firehouse—which was only four houses away from his. As he approached an emergency medical technician, Morrison began explaining the urgent situation. Instead of alerting the crews on site, the technician then recommended that Morrison call 911 instead.

Morrison had no phone and told the man that if he looked down the street he could see the blaze coming from his roof. The technician was unsympathetic and closed the door on him. With the help of his neighbors, the 911 call was finally placed. Emergency crews took eight minutes to respond.

The emergency medical technician was later interviewed, and authorities claim that Morrison's account was false because the EMT has a "good record" from his long standing employment with the department. Unfortunately, due to lack of empathy, Morrison's home was completely destroyed by the blaze. No one was hurt, but someone in the department should have been reprimanded for their stupid and insensitive response to an emergency.

# CHAPTER 2:
# CRIME GONE WRONG

Criminals aren't the smartest bunch of people. And they're not the most trustworthy people either. Most recidivists are scheming for their next opportunity all the time, although they may not be thinking their plan the whole way through.  Every little unsecured door or window is logged into their list of future opportunities. Every little glimmer of gold and riches is pursued with tunnel vision. Sometimes they actually make it out to the light at the end of the tunnel and sometimes their dreams are truncated by flashing red and blue lights.

Criminals believe that the law doesn't apply to them, but it does. When the swift punishment of law enforcement catches up with them, there is no place to go but toward punitive institutions filled with like-minded people who lack the foresight to keep themselves out of said places in the first place. You might be amazed at what some criminals think they can get away with these days, but it's more amazing that law enforcement is able to catch these offenders in the middle of their stupidity-filled acts. Stories of crime gone wrong give us so much to talk and laugh about, because we learn that some people really don't know where the line falls between the legal and the illegal.

# CRIMINALS WHO COULDN'T COVER THEIR TRACKS

*What is the perfect crime? Can it exist? Is the perfect crime the crime with no evidence leading back to it? If you can't find evidence for a crime, did the crime even occur? How can we say a crime has happened when there is no evidence of the crime?*

*These questions have plagued investigators on the case of the world's smartest criminals, criminals who leave no tracks in their wake. But not all criminals are geniuses. Actually, most of them aren't. The median level of education for most criminals might not that be that high, but it doesn't take much education for investigators to follow their trail of evidence either.*

*In some cases, criminals may have run out of time to cover their tracks, and in others, they might not have realized that they were breaking the law because it was just so much a part of their everyday lives. Who knows what happens in the mind of a criminal? Although you may never know, one thing is for sure: they sure do like to look for money in the homes and places of employment of other people.*

## A CRIMINAL'S PROFILE

There are certain situations where using social media is okay—like when you're bored at home or on the train—and there are other situations in which it isn't. A man from Minneapolis, Minnesota, James Wood, came home one evening to find a wet pair of pants on the floor, a strange Facebook account logged in on his computer, and his home burglarized. Wood noticed credit cards, cash, and other valuables missing from his home, along with a general mess from the broken glass and rain coming in from outside. Wood had been burglarized, and lucky for him, he had everything he needed for justice.

The dimwitted thief left his Facebook account open on Wood's computer, giving Wood the opportunity to express his anger and seek justice. Wood wrote a scathing message with his phone number on the criminal's wall, and—surprisingly—the criminal texted him a few hours later.

Wood told the thief that he had left a few things at his house, and that they should meet so Wood could return the thief's belongings. The next day they met to exchange the left behind goods, but before the thief got his items, he got what he deserved. Upon arriving to the rendezvous point, Wood recognized the criminal from his Facebook photo and immediately called the cops, who arrested the man and charged him with second-degree burglary.

## CAR THIEF LOOKING TO MAKE SOME FAST CASH

A car thief in Albany, New York, made away with a 2007 PT Cruiser and the car owner's cell phone in hopes to make some fast cash. The car owner began to call his phone frantically after realizing the fate of his car and his belongings in it. After several tries, the car thief, fifty-five-year-old David Moore, finally answered, ready to make a deal.

Moore knew that the car would—if it wasn't already—be reported to the police as stolen, and that it would only be a matter of time before the law caught up with him. Moore wanted to make a deal. He told the owner of the car that he would return the car in exchange for $20, and that they should meet to do the exchange.

Maybe a little outside of Moore's strategic foresight, the owner of the car had no plans to pay Moore the $20 they had agreed upon. Probably a predictable situation for most, but Moore didn't see what was coming.

The car owner stayed true to his word by meeting Moore, but he didn't bring the money with him. Instead, the owner had Albany's finest escort him into the situation to arrest this shortsighted car thief. It's no joke when people say that crime doesn't pay, especially when it's only $20.

## GOT TO CATCH THEM ALL

It seems like thieves have a problem with keeping track of their possessions while stealing from other people. A comic book store in Festus, Missouri, was recently robbed of two Kiss action figures, Pokemon cards, a laptop, $35 in cash, and the store's cash register.

Jason Hughes and Brandon Williams, the store owners, told police that the store was broken in through the back entryway and that the burglar had left behind—in true geek-fandom fashion—a calling card of sorts. They had found a pack of cigarettes and the criminal's phone that rang multiple times—flashing the criminal's face on the locked screen—as the police investigated the scene.

The cell phone eventually led to the arrest of the criminal and the return of the merchandise to the store. All Pokemon were returned safely into the care of the storeowners.

### GOOGLE SEARCH: POLICE NEAR ME

Horatio Toure was on a bike ride in the Market neighborhood of San Francisco, California, looking for an unlucky victim he could snatch a phone from. He found his target and began to pedal his way toward her location, waiting for the perfect time to cruise by and swipe her phone from her hands.

Unlucky for Toure, the woman was working for her company, testing a real-time GPS tracking application. Toure snatched the phone and fled, but didn't get far before he was caught.

The application was the only application running on the phone, making it awfully easy to see where he went to hide with his smart-phone loot. The police followed the application to Toure, who was logging into his email account on the phone. Toure was booked in jail for suspicion of grand theft and possession of stolen property.

## ICE COLD FUGITIVE

Most of the time, it's a standup thing to raise money for fundraisers, but maybe it isn't too smart to do so on social media when you're a wanted fugitive. A man from Omaha, Nebraska, Jesean Morris, should have known better than to film himself participating in the ALS Ice Bucket Challenge and post it on Facebook, but he didn't.

Wanting to be a part of this philanthropic online sensation, Morris led police right to his door with the evidence found in his ice-bucket video. Police examined the video and determined the area in which Morris had been living under the radar of the law. Police began to hone in on their fugitive's location.

With the help of an informant who knew of Morris' past, police were given the exact address where Morris had been staying. They watched Morris and his house for some time until they made their move as he entered the back of a friend's car that then drove off. The officers pulled the car over and arrested Morris, who was still not thrilled by the prospect of cold cells and showers in the local penitentiary. One thing is obvious, not even ice can cool down the hot trail of evidence found on the social-media profiles of criminals.

## MACARONI SALAD FOR THREE

Even though you break into a restaurant to steal its cash register and surveillance system, it doesn't mean that there is no evidence leading back to you. Mt. Morris, New York, restaurant Build-A-Burger received justice when three burglars—who stole various electronics, cash, and a big bowl of macaroni salad—were arrested after their trail of evidence led the cops straight to them.

The cops arrived on the scene of the restaurant to begin their investigation when they discovered a trail of cash register parts, rubber gloves, and macaroni salad along the pedestrian trail behind the restaurant. After following the evidence for a short time, the trail of evidence led to the hungry burglars' hideout.

Arrested for the offense was M. Sapetko, thirty-four, J. Marullo, thirty-five, and T. Walker, twenty-three, who were later charged with fourth-degree grand larceny, third-degree burglary, and third-degree criminal mischief. According to the police report, the three men passed around the bowl of macaroni salad to eat as they escaped, leaving a mess of evidence behind them.

Although all of the other merchandise was returned to the restaurant, the macaroni salad had to be thrown away. That night, the three men were able to fall asleep in jail with their bellies full of their last meal as free men for many years to come.

## THEY ALMOST GOT AWAY WITH WHAT?

*People are confounding. What makes them do the things—illegal or not—that they do? What might seem to be one of the best ideas to one is the most stupid idea to another. One man's trash may be another's treasure, but one man's cash can always become the cash of another. It's all relative, but most people can recognize the sheer stupidity of some situations.*

*From squatting in an elderly woman's house to explaining your conniving crime to your father in front of investigating police, these are some of the worst scenarios you can get yourself into because they could have easily been prevented. Just like before, you may have never known about these crimes if the criminals weren't caught, but if they weren't caught, you'd have nothing to laugh about. Let's give it up not only for the criminals with imaginative and grandiose schemes, but also for their inability to predict the impending doom of those plots.*

## STAYING AT GRANDMA'S HOUSE

An eighty-year-old Pennsylvanian woman thought she had been living alone in her two-story house in Bedford, but it turns out she was mistaken. Police on the case claim that a forty-nine-year-old man was secretly living upstairs in the woman's house for weeks before he was found. His little holiday was truncated when the woman's daughter came to visit and heard a suspicious noise coming from upstairs. Upon further investigation, Mark Allen Potts was found hiding in a closet.

Police found duffel bags, suitcases, personal belongings, and a handgun in the upstairs room where Potts was staying, and then charged him with criminal trespassing. The gun was supposedly Potts' protection from trespassers, but it did no good in protecting him from the investigative mother and daughter team. During the arrest, the woman recognized the trespasser as her former caretaker's boyfriend. It might not be good to find people squatting in your house, but one thing is for sure, it's never a good thing when you get to know your caretaker's boyfriend.

## DRUG TRAFFICKING IN TRAFFIC COURT

Sometimes the line between bravery and stupidity is awfully obscure, and you just can't tell if criminals are truly fearless or if they're truly clueless. A Glenshaw, Pennsylvania, man, Christopher Durkin, was in traffic court for one count of driving on a suspended license and ended up leaving that day with a few more counts against him.

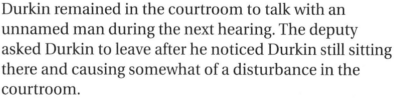

Durkin sat patiently through his court hearing, waiting for his punishment. After the conclusion of his hearing, Durkin remained in the courtroom to talk with an unnamed man during the next hearing. The deputy asked Durkin to leave after he noticed Durkin still sitting there and causing somewhat of a disturbance in the courtroom.

Durkin left peacefully and everyone thought that was the end of that, but the unnamed man then confessed that Durkin had just tried to sell him the narcotic Suboxone —a prescription used to help opioid addicts deal with withdrawal symptoms.

Durkin hadn't gotten far when the deputy stopped him and searched him, finding two doses of the prescription drug on him and charging him with intent to distribute and possession of a controlled substance. Although Durkin was dreaming of hitting the open road with a valid license, he was unable to work his way around this traffic jam.

## FRENCH ASSURANCE

A break-and-enter scene in Calgary, Alberta, had all the signs of a real crime scene—missing electronics and jewelry, a hysterical victim, smashed windows, and dirty footprints leading away from the scene. Everything seemed to add up to a robbery that left the victims with nothing, but as the case unraveled, the victims turned out to be the criminals.

Everything at the scene started to make sense as Constable Charanjit Meharu arrived and began interviewing one of the victims. The victim's phone rang, and she asked the constable to excuse her while she answered a call from her father. The victim spoke Quebecois French to her father, explaining everything that had happened, but what she was telling her father was not what she had told the constable. Const. Meharu spoke seven different languages, and that day, his French lessons were paying off.

The victim—not knowing the constable was a polyglot and well versed in French—began explaining her and her boyfriend's plot to make a fraud insurance claim for some extra cash. She explained over the phone how they had hid all of their jewelry and electronics, smashed their windows, and even planted fake footprints leading away from the home. She reassured him that law enforcement was buying it.

Slowly, the victims' machinations unraveled, revealing the couple not as victims but as perpetrators. As the phone call ended, Const. Meharu put away his ten pages of notes he had just taken from the phone call and said, "Merci beaucoup," startling the woman with the fact that he understood every word she said. The couple was charged with mischief.

## FLORIDA WOMAN'S NAME JUST A RANDOM STRING OF WORDS

A group of fraudulent shoppers were charged with buying a spear gun and a digital camera from a local surf shop in Jupiter, Florida. Paying for their merchandise with a declined credit card, the group of three twenty-year-olds were later detained by police for fraud.

The report was later shared on the *Florida Woman* Twitter account because of the name of the woman who took part in the crime. Cherries Waffles Tennis was charged with her two male friends for fraud and was then made a mockery of because of her seemingly random-string-of-words name.

Cherries Waffles Tennis is now part of the Florida elite who are talked about on the ridiculous-but-true social-media sites of *Florida Man* and *Florida Woman*. Although Cherries Waffles Tennis might not be the most absurd story this entertainment site has talked about, she sure has the most absurd name anyone has seen.

## ILL-THOUGHT SCHEMES

*Most people refrain from crime when they realize how easily they can be caught. Even when you can't see the evidence, investigators can search at microscopic scales to find anything that might lead them on the right track. That thought alone—and, well, having a good conscience too—will stop almost everyone from pulling off that one big jewelry heist or bank robbery.*

*But some people don't think of these things whatsoever. They don't think about the DNA evidence left behind in infinitesimal amounts of hair or skin, they don't think about the database of information law enforcement units have to refer to, they don't think about everything that is working against them in pulling off the perfect crime. Some criminals don't think their actions through at all, making it pretty obvious that a crime has been committed and who it was committed by.*

*It is a rare occurrence for a criminal to actually achieve that one big deal, but if they used a little bit of precaution, they might have been able to give themselves a little extra time to run. Using a little bit of foresight won't guarantee that you won't get caught, but at least it won't make you look like a fool after you attempt your ridiculous and ill-thought scheme.*

## MIAMI ICE

Miami Police arrested a man who held up a local Checkers restaurant for cash and customers' jewelry. Early that morning as the restaurant was opening, the Florida man jumped out of the storage freezer and began his heist. The customers ran outside to safety, calling 911 in hopes that the police would get there in time. They did, and the man was arrested for third-degree burglary.

The puzzling thing for the cops working the case is how long the man waited in the freezer before he began his heist. It could have been an hour or a few, but it certainly wasn't all night because it is likely the man would have frozen to death before he had a chance to make his move.

## HAMBURGLARS FOILED BY THE KING

Two men from Stockton, California, attempted to rob a Burger King but had trouble finding their get-away car afterwards. The two criminals, J. Lovitt and G. Gonzales, entered the burger joint with their guns out and loaded at 9:45 p.m. The two men focused on one crew member and the manager to get their loot as— unbeknownst to them—the third employee snuck out the back entrance of the restaurant.

Lovitt and Gonzales packed their sacks with cash as quickly as possible in order to get back to their running getaway car parked out back, but what they didn't realize was that their car wouldn't be waiting for them. As the third employee snuck out back to call the cops, he noticed a running car that he figured belonged to the burglars. The quick-thinking employee jumped in the car and drove it around the corner, leaving the ham-burglars without a fast-food escape route.

The two came running outside only to realize that their plan had been foiled. They ran around the parking lot frantically, looking for their car, but to no avail. Lovitt and Gonzales fled on foot but were soon apprehended by the Stockton Police and taken to San Joaquin County Jail. Maybe they'll be smart enough to use Grimace as a getaway driver the next time they decide to mess with the king of burgers.

### FORGING FAME

Charles Ray Fuller, a twenty-one-year-old North Texan, had big dreams of being a record producer and owning his own record label. He had the drugs and the guns, and now all he needed was the cash. He had a plan. He would take a check from his girlfriend's mother, fill it out, cash it in, and start his path toward pop royalty. He thought about how much money he should start with. $1,000? $25,000? Nah, how about a nice even $360 billion! That sure does seem reasonable for a fledging company, doesn't it?

It wasn't Fuller's sketchy attitude or shady character that tipped off the tellers, but the fact that there were ten zeros following the numerals on this personal check.

Maybe Fuller didn't know, but not many people are cashing in personal checks for hundreds of billions of dollars at their local Wells Fargo branch. Suspicious of the transaction, the tellers contacted the account's owner to verify if the check was legitimate—which it wasn't. His girlfriend's mother never gave him permission to take any of her money or checks, and—so—the police arrived to deal with the situation.

Aside from the charges of forgery, Fuller was also busted for his other record-label supplies. The cops found a .25-caliber handgun and just under two ounces of marijuana in Fuller's pant pockets. Fuller's dreams of lounging on the throne of fame came crashing down, and at that moment, he knew that he'd have to start—once again—from the bottom to reach his dreams.

## WANTED CRIMINALS WIN FREE CASES OF BEER

The Derbyshire Police Department of England had quite a few fugitives they couldn't get a grip on. The fugitives had evaded all of the law enforcement's previous tactics to bring them into custody, but there was one thing the fugitives couldn't resist: free beer.

Although it seemed far-fetched, calling these wanted criminals and saying they won a case of free beer with a fake sweepstakes ploy was the detectives' only hope to bring these fugitives to justice. Undercover agents called the criminals with the faux news and arranged a time and a place in which they could come and pick up their free case of beer. Many were intrigued, but not all of them fell for the trap.

All in all, nineteen thirsty fugitives arrived and were then brought in to the station, realizing that the free beer they were promised would never come to materialize. One thing that did materialize in Derbyshire that day was the swift and cunning stratagems of law enforcement.

## NEVER LOSE SLEEP OVER GUILT

A man from Manchester, New Hampshire, woke up to a strange sight one morning in the home he shared with his wife. Walking into the hallway after a quiet night's sleep, John Terrell found a random pair of shoes outside of an unoccupied bedroom.

A little shocked by the confusing placement of a pair of shoes he had never seen before, he peeked through the open door to find a man sleeping in the bed with a large hunting knife sticking out of his back pocket. John grabbed the pair of shoes and quietly walked back to the bedroom where his wife was still sleeping. He woke her, and she couldn't believe what he told her until she saw the pair of shoes. It was startling, but they were calm as Elinor Terrell called the police and John held the man at gunpoint.

Apparently, the burglar, Renaud Plaisir, had been on an all-night spree and was pretty tired by time he got to the

Terrell's home. Plaisir cut a hole in the screen door on the first floor, searched through the downstairs cabinetry, scavenged some leftover hot wings from the fridge, made his way upstairs, and fell into bed for a little cat nap.

Plaisir missed his alarm though. When the police arrived, they found a backpack full of merchandise from homes he had hit earlier in the night. Plaisir had apparently made it through the whole house perusing it for valuables, but he was never able to make it out. He woke in the morning—not  knowing where he was—to police officers swarming around him. Plaisir was taken in and charged with burglary.

# CHAPTER 3:
# BAD DRIVERS AND EVEN WORSE DRIVING

Automobiles are some of the most dangerous everyday items of the 20th century. A tiny one hundred and eighty pound pedestrian has no chance to survive if they were to take a two-ton automobile head on—they might leave a dent, but that's all they'd leave behind. Your average drive around the countryside is dangerous enough, but add erratic and impatient drivers, lead feet, distractions from ever-evolving smartphones, and an increased number of pedestrians and the situation becomes much more dangerous.

In the U.S. alone, tens of thousands of deaths occur from traffic accidents, while tens of thousands of others are injured in car crashes every year. It is easy to forget in the isolated space of your car that you are manning a dangerous weapon that careens through the streets at high speeds. You turn on your favorite playlist, roll down the windows, and hit the road without a worry on your mind, but the chances of an accident are far higher than you would like to admit. Go on, admit it; you tend to become a little careless in the unwarranted protection of your car.

People never shy away from finding new uses or places for their car. You can look away from the road for a second and find a lovely spot to park your car wedged between two traffic medians. You can push your engine to the limit when you have an insatiable desire to go fast. You can speed around the city trying to make it on time to the next appointment of your packed schedule and break any number of laws along the way. Driving sure isn't the safest thing you can do, but it sure is one of the most fun. And although it may be fun, it only becomes more dangerous as you use your car more and more for jammed commutes to work—letting the anger and frustration build up—instead of careless summer joyrides.

## LOCALS TRAVELING FASTER THAN ALLOWED

*Nothing is more fun to do in your car than to travel at high rates of speed. You can hit 60 mph in a matter of seconds with a lot of cars these days, and you can push your engine to the limit as your RPMs redline in the seven thousands. It is a thrill that man before modern times never knew—except for maybe riding a really fast horse, but that doesn't compare to driving a fast car. It may be fun and exhilarating but it's also a super obvious way to tell law enforcement that you're breaking the law. There isn't much guesswork involved in determining if a car is going too fast or not when you see it zip past you. It's not like you can hit the brakes and make it back down to the speed limit just a few feet before you pass the cop sitting on the side of the road. It doesn't work that way—and it's probably better that it doesn't. People are pulled over for speeding all the time, but most of them never seem to learn their lesson. These locals are great examples of why you should always stay below the speed limit, because the repercussions grow exponentially with every additional mile per hour.*

## TWO TICKETS TO RIDE

Some people have a need for speed, and some people just never learn. Royalton, Vermont, resident Seth Tichenor is a person who falls neatly into both categories.

Tichenor was running late for traffic court to resolve a speeding ticket. He started on his way and hit the interstate, but he just couldn't catch up to his schedule. He kept adding a little more pressure to the gas pedal every time he passed someone, eventually making his way up to 112 mph in a 65 mph zone.

He was getting closer and closer and faster and faster every second, cutting his time down to the bone, until he saw those red and blue lights flashing in his rearview mirror.

The interstate patrolman didn't only issue a ticket this time; Tichenor was nearly going double the speed limit! He wasn't charged with a petty moving violation but severe speeding charges and time spent in a jail cell. Tichenor was charged with excessive speed and negligent operation. He was later released to take care of his original speeding ticket.

## NEVER MIND THE GATEKEEPER

This report is a nice segue from speeding locals to reckless locals because it takes a little bit of both to create such a mess. A twenty-two-year-old San Francisco man, Daniel Micah Soto, had a hard time getting over the Golden Gate Bridge in his new Ford Mustang, crashing through security gates and careening onto the pedestrian path. Officials claim that as Soto approached the security gate on the bridge, he hit the gas, moving at an incredible amount of speed not normally seen approaching the bridge.

Soto drove through the gate while turning into the parking lot, and then continued onto the sidewalk, plowing through another gate and a steel gate. After that, he made it another couple of hundred yards before wedging his car in between the chain-link fence and the guardrail of the pedestrian path usually reserved for bicyclists.

Soto was sent to the hospital for injuries suffered from the deployment of his airbags, while his Mustang was left behind as bridge workers contemplated how to remove it from its tightly wedged position. Fortunately, the bridge workers love puzzles, because they sure got one.

## BROADCAST YOURSELF DOING
## THE DUMBEST THINGS

I think we all—or most of us—know better than to associate any illegal activity we might participate in with our social media accounts, but eighteen-year-old Robert Kelley didn't. Kelley was so proud of his reckless driving that he posted the video of his joyride to social media as he lay hospitalized from it.

The video of the Smyrna Beach resident weaving between cars, blowing red lights and stop signs, speeding, and jamming out to some hardcore techno music is almost as good as the latest *The Fast and the Furious* movie except it ends with a crash.

Kelley drove ceaselessly like an idiot, not letting anything—including traffic laws—stand in his way. He crashed into one car, but that didn't stop him. Speeding down the Florida roads, Kelley then ran into three more cars in one accident that left him injured and his car totaled. Kelley had to be cut from his car and then airlifted to the hospital. Others involved in the crash were also injured.

The next day while he was in the hospital, Kelley posted the video of his reckless driving—which he apparently filmed in true idiocy—to YouTube, giving officers a few more offenses on their list of charges. Kelley was ultimately charged with fleeing the scene of an accident with injuries, reckless driving, and driving without a license.

# LOCALS DRIVING INTO STUFF

*Most people can be a little clumsy sometimes. There are those times when you are dead tired and sore and you sort of stumble around the house trying to get yourself a glass of water, and then you stub your toe on the doorframe and drop the glass and then—as you jump up and down holding your toe—you begin a painful one-footed dance on top of the broken glass. Most people do that sometimes, right? Well, maybe some people aren't that clumsy, but that situation has nothing on the clumsy, reckless, and heavy-footed locals who couldn't help but drive their cars into something they shouldn't have.*

## PANCAKING THE WAFFLE HOUSE

A Florida woman drove into the side of a Waffle House restaurant as she tried to park her car in the surrounding parking lot. The forty-four-year-old woman—with a pretty good buzz going that evening—was obviously very excited to get breakfast for dinner at this roadside staple. Her hunger, excitement, and inebriation caused her to jump the curb and crash into the outside wall of the restaurant.

She would have been able to get away from the wreckage and flee if it weren't for two nearby sheriff's deputies who had heard the crash. Upon their arrival, they stopped the woman from fleeing the scene and soon realized her condition.

As they told her to exit the vehicle, they noticed her lack of pants and how much difficulty she had standing on her own. The deputies had a pretty good idea of what was going on by that point, but first took her to the hospital to treat the injuries she sustained during her close encounter with the Waffle House. After her condition stabilized, the deputies charged her with a DUI for a blood alcohol level of .295 and property damage for pancaking the Waffle House.

## COLD-BLOODED CRASH AND BURN

One might have expected a plume of smoke to exit the Smoke N Toke Lounge when a Hialeah, Florida, woman crashed into its glass entryway in April of 2016, but there wasn't. What did come crawling out of the smoke-shop was the store's collection of exotic reptiles.

The situation leading up to the crash is still unclear, but one thing is for sure, the woman definitely overshot her parking space. The woman and her child did not sustain injuries from the crash, but numerous snakes and lizards escaped as their glass enclosures were broken along with the store's front window. Many of the reptiles were recovered, but four were never found.

## PORTLAND RESIDENT DITCHES CAR TO BECOME A PEDESTRIAN

Many cities throughout the U.S. are currently undertaking projects to make their streets friendlier to pedestrians. Portland, Oregon, recently finished renovations on its Sellwood Bridge that created a designated section for walkers, runners, and cyclists to cross the bridge safely, but not everyone knew that cars were not permitted.

An abandoned truck created a dead end for many pedestrians one day as they crossed the bridge. The unknown resident must have been confused after the construction ended and made their way down to the newly renovated section of the bridge, quickly realizing they were definitely in the wrong place. The driver drove down the entryway of the pedestrian path, but didn't even try to turn around.

We're not quite sure what happened with the driver, but we can imagine. The driver of the truck probably made their way down to the area and noticed that their truck was a sore thumb out amongst all of the people traveling by the power of their own two feet. The driver must have gotten a little nervous with no way to back out of the area, so they decided to take a hint, get out of their car, and run with the pack.

The vehicle was abandoned directly in front of the path entrance, blocking anyone from entering or exiting, leading many cyclists to dismount, pick up their bikes, climb over traffic barricades, and dodge oncoming traffic to make it to the other exit. Others just turned around and made their way over to the Ross Island Bridge. Either way it was a throwback to the less-pedestrian-friendly days where car dodging and barricade jumping were regular routines for pedestrians. We can only imagine the day when police catch up with this driver turned pedestrian to ask them what really happened when they abandoned their car on the bridge.

## DRIVE-THRU LICENSE CENTER

A Pennsylvania man was about to pass his driving test; then he crashed into the front entrance of the Driving License Center in the Chartiers Valley Shopping Area. The instructor was one check mark away from completing his examination before the driver—in one fell swoop—failed for good.

The student driver, thrity-four-year-old Robert Keller, had done so well on the road, but when it came to test his parking skills he couldn't help but hit the gas in a fit of anxiety. The report claims that Keller made it all the way back to the driving center without a hitch, but as it came time to park, he forgot to put the car in park. The car then jumped the curb and Keller panicked, hitting the gas pedal instead of the brakes and launching the car into the building's glass front entrance.

A student driver, waiting for his license inside the building, was surprised to hear such a commotion inside the quiet driving center. He was scared by the uproar and immediately turned to see the car careening into the building and people jumping out of the way. Four people were mildly injured and taken to the hospital for an evaluation of their abrasions.

Keller and the instructor were fine but still a little shaken from the grand and unexpected entrance. Keller—completely embarrassed—kept apologizing for the slip up and was not charged by the police. Understandably, he did not pass the test and did not receive his license.

## HOLD ON KIDS, WE'RE GOING OVER!

Anyone who drives in a big city knows all of the shortcuts when they're running late during rush hour. A father who was behind in dropping his kids off in the morning knew all of the shortcuts. He sped down alleyways, used the left-hand lane as a passing lane, and cut through parking lots to forgo red lights regularly, but eventually, he came across an obstacle that stopped him right in his tracks.

Dashing to his kids' school, a Brampton, Ontario, man cut through a corner parking lot to avoid a red light when he ran over two recently installed posts to prevent people from cutting through. The man's Nissan SUV went over the first post, bending the barricade to a forty-five degree angle, which then acted as a ramp for the car to then continue to the next post where the undercarriage of the car got stuck. The car's front-end dove back to the ground as the back-end was held off the ground by the second post—still stuck under the car.

The car's nosedive did some damage to the front fender, but the two posts did considerable damage to the underside of the car as it dangled there waiting for a special tow truck to take it away. After all of that scheming, mapping, coordinating, and effort to get the kids to school on time for once, they were still late that day.

## DRIVERS ACROSS THE WORLD HAVE BEEN CONFIRMED AS DUMB

*Although you may feel completely free within the confines of your car, you're not. Some people get a little too comfy in their car and start to get used to doing stupid stuff while they're in it. No, you shouldn't let your dog take the wheel. No, you shouldn't load two trucks into the back of another truck. No, just no! The things some people almost get away with in their car makes you wonder what people actually do get away with in their cars. If these are the stories of the people who were caught by cops doing dumb stuff, imagine all of the people who were never caught. Despite all of the stupid stuff these stupid drivers have done, you can be assured that there is someone out there who was never caught for driving while doing something infinitely more stupid. Let's hope that law enforcement starts cracking down on these dumb drivers more often.*

## OKAY, NOW KEEP BOTH PAWS ON THE WHEEL!

A woman was recently reprimanded for letting her Yorkshire terrier take the wheel of her Toyota sedan while driving on a road near Llanelli, South Wales. Passengers in passing vehicles were awestruck and astonished to see a feisty terrier with both paws on the wheel of a car moving at 30 mph.

The passing cars snapped photos of the terrier at the wheel and sent it to local officials because of the danger it posed to the public. For one thing, there is no need for dogs to be driving cars, let alone hyperactive terriers with aggression problems.

Using the photos, local authorities were able to track the car's registration and address to investigate the situation further. The owner of the car and motor-skilled dog confessed to letting the dog take the wheel and now promises to keep the dog in the back of the car while driving.

## PACK THE HEAVY STUFF FIRST

A Chinese man in the province of Shanxi gave us a whole new idea to the phrase "traffic pileup" as he drove three trucks stacked atop each other down a provincial freeway. The man loaded the smallest of the three trucks into the bed of the second truck, and then loaded the second truck—with the smallest truck in its bed—into the bed of the largest truck like a set of finely crafted Russian nesting dolls.

The driver might have been inspired by the Russian toys, but he was motivated by economics. He claimed that he got the idea because he was trying to avoid pricey shipping costs, which he ended having to pay anyway after the patrolman stopped him on the freeway. The patrolman was not amused by this man's resourcefulness and gave him a ¥ 200 ($30) violation and required him to ship the trucks individually.

China, an industrial powerhouse, is no stranger to creative solutions to shipping problems. Other violations have been reported throughout the country of similar hauls. An instance in the province of Anhui one-upped the Shanxi three-truck pileup with a total haul of five trucks—a truck with two other trucks loaded into its bed while also towing another truck with a truck in its bed. You'd think that with the size of China's population that there would be plenty of people to drive these trucks individually, but instances of trucks packed with trucks continue to occur on a regular basis in this overcrowded country.

## DO NOT CROSS WHEN FLOODED

Most would assume that a state as arid as Arizona would not have to worry about water flooding its highways, but when it rains, it pours, and when the rivers run, they run many feet deep. Flash-flooding occurs frequently when parts of the state receive large storms, causing water to torrentially run down the mountain sides and into the washes of lower lying valleys and canyons. The flooded washes run like Rocky Mountain white-water rivers for many hours and create a great threat to motorists trying to cross them.

Although horror stories of flash-flooding are prevalent in the area, you still hear of overly confident, albeit stupid, drivers who try to ford the rushing waters. For those unstoppable drivers, Arizona has upheld the Stupid Motorist Law since 1995 to discourage them from crossing flooded washes.

One monsoon season, an instance in Scottsdale, Arizona, left two local men stranded in a van amongst the rising desert floodwaters of the Indian Bend Wash. Although barricades and warning signs blocked the road from passing motorists, the two men continued past the warnings and attempted to cross the wash. Inevitably, their van was stopped in its tracks as its engine flooded out. With nowhere to go, the men quickly realized their almost fatal mistake.

Emergency personnel arrived to save the day at a $4,000 cost, using a ladder for the men to traverse the waters to safety. Upon reaching dry land, the men were cited as "stupid motorists" by the Scottsdale Police and were charged an additional $2,000 in fines. Lucky for them, a helicopter was not needed for the rescue, which would have tacked on an additional $2,000 per hour to the many thousands of dollars they were already paying for their hasty mistake.

## THE ENGLISH DRIVE ON THE WRONG SIDE OF THE ROAD

Lane closures on England's M65 motorway might have confused the flow of traffic, leading fifty different vehicles to go the wrong direction in the face of oncoming cars. The police that night were forced to close M65 due to reports of a man walking along the motorway, but they were soon to face many more people than they expected in an area they were not supposed to be.

During the lane closure for this lone pedestrian, more than fifty motorists decided to flip a U-turn on the highway, go the wrong way, and exit on a side street. These dumb, dangerous, and irresponsible drivers not only put their own lives at risk, but also risked the lives of other motorists correctly travelling the right direction on the motorway.

Unfortunate for the drivers going the wrong way, the lanes were reopened to traffic on the opposite side of the road—led by a fleet of police cars. The drivers going the wrong way were met by a phalanx of blue lights. All fifty motorists were charged with a hefty fine and will possibly be disqualified from driving.

### FIRING ON ALL CYLINDERS

Having your car towed is one of the worst surprises we can encounter in this day and age. There is nothing like coming out of a concert or restaurant in the most trendy part of town—laughing and enjoying your time thoroughly—to find that you had parked your car illegally, and it had been towed away while you were gone. There might not be much you can do once your car is up on the tow-truck but there is one thing you can do to bring it back down to the street.

A forty-year-old Manchester, New Hampshire, man thought of a brilliant way to stop the tow-truck driver from towing his car away. Shad Badeau had illegally parked his car, and by time he came back, the tow-truck driver already had his car on the truck and was ready to drive off. Badeau thought about how to stop this from happening and came up with the perfect idea: light the car on fire so it couldn't be towed.

The car went up in flames fairly quickly, causing the tow-truck driver to drop the car back down and unhitch it. Badeau put out the fire after the car was back on the street, but his plan didn't go down without a hitch. The Manchester Police arrived and charged Badeau with arson. No word has been given whether the car was later towed away or not.

## COLORING WITHIN THE LINES LEADS TO PARKING WITHIN THE LINES

An American man has been fighting back against people who take up multiple parking spaces with a childhood lesson that just might teach them to stay within the lines.

It is a common occurrence for people to pull into a parking lot of a local strip mall to find privileged drivers taking more space than they need to protect their cars from being dinged. What isn't common is for anyone to do anything about it. Well, except for one man.

Peeved by these excessive parkers, a local Florida man has been leaving notes on the windshields of these cars to help them stay within the lines. The man leaves a coloring book page of a turtle with a nice note that suggests if a three-year-old can color within the lines, then they can too. Coloring a turtle shouldn't be as hard as parking within the lines, but many people still have trouble with it.

The note might seem passive-aggressive, but it's a better solution than the aggressive tactics of letting air out of tires or scraping keys along the car's paint job. Many people have to deal with these childish drivers that take up more space than they need, but now we all have a good way to treat them like the children they are. Coloring within the lines of a coloring book is now recommended for many privileged folks to pass their driving test.

## WOMAN EXPOSES MORE THAN SHE WANTED TO

A woman from Elyria, Ohio, forty-nine-year-old Elizabeth Johnson, thought she might be able to get out of a traffic stop by showing a little skin, but she ended up exposing more than she wanted. What turned out to be a normal traffic stop turned into a peep show and then a drug bust.

Reports say that early that morning, Johnson was pulled over for a standard traffic violation, but the officer became suspicious after he watched her reach into her shirt as if she were stashing something in her bra. The officer ordered Johnson out of the car, but she did not cooperate.

Johnson locked the doors of her car and rolled up her windows, refusing to come out to speak to the officer. She became erratic, yelling at the officer and still not cooperating.

Reports claim that the officer eventually convinced Johnson to come out of her car, but she was no calmer than before. She screamed and screamed, finally saying, "Fine, you want to see what I have," as she lifted up her shirt.

Johnson pulled her shirt and her bra up over her head, exposing her breasts to the officer, trying to prove that she wasn't hiding anything. But her plan didn't go as she suspected, because she forgot to secure what she was actually hiding in her bra.

The bra and shirt went up, but her crack pipe fell to the ground. The officer told her to cover herself and immediately picked up the pipe to collect as evidence against Johnson.

Johnson was arrested and charged with possession of cocaine, obstructing official business, and possession of drug paraphernalia.

# DISTRACTED AND/OR INEBRIATED

*There can be a whole book written on all of the things that can distract you from the road. First off, there is the smartphone that actually engages us more than talking to another human face-to-face. And even after that, talking to someone in the passenger seat is pretty darn distracting as well. You could be talking to your passenger about the controversial topics of Internet privacy or gun control and totally miss your turn on the highway—which really isn't that bad of a situation. Or you could drop your cigarette between the seat and the console, reach down frantically to try to save it from burning the upholstery, and look up to see that you're going to rear-end the car in front of you. Don't even consider all the other distractions that come along when you've had a few to drink. Consider these stories to be a list of things not to be distracted by the next time you get inside of your car.*

## DRIVING THE MESSAGE THROUGH

Texting while driving can be a serious road hazard. It can preoccupy drivers enraptured by deep conversations filled with contractions, emojis, memes, and selfies. It can take a driver's hands and eyes off the road for many seconds, leading to catastrophic crashes and downright horrible driving.

A Maryland woman recently reminded us of how important it is to not text and drive when she ended up hitting a tree and driving into a lake. The woman lost control of her Hyundai on the road as she texted "OMG!"

to a friend, not referring to what was about to happen but in response to her friend's gossip.

In the middle of her heartfelt text-athon, the woman smacked into a tree and then drove another sixty feet straight into Waldorf Lake. Diving right in, the car ended up submerged under five feet of water. "OMG, OMG!" the woman yelled as her car began to sink.

Lucky for her, her run in with the tree busted her window out, which allowed her to safely exit the sinking vehicle. Police have charged her with reckless driving and probably should have banned her from her smartphone as well. This has been a helpful reminder to keep your eyes on the road and off the screen.

## GONE FISHIN'

Wisconsin is known for its beer, country roads, and fish fries. What happens when you add the three together? You get an everyday situation with an outlandish explanation. A seventy-six-year-old Wisconsin man, John Przybyla, faced his tenth charge of operating a vehicle while intoxicated because of—as he claimed—the beer battered fish he had eaten earlier that night for dinner.

A deputy had noticed Przybyla's car swerving across the centerline of a county road while patrolling the Wisconsin countryside. The deputy approached the car and immediately smelled alcohol on Przybyla's breath. A field sobriety test was conducted.

Przybyla failed and explained that the reason why he smelled and acted like he was under the influence was because he had eaten beer battered fish for dinner. The deputy laughed and asked how much beer battered fish one would have to eat to act and smell the way Przybyla did that evening. Apparently, Przybyla had eaten so much beer battered fish that his blood alcohol level was nearly .06, which is under the legal limit in Wisconsin unless you are a repeat offender—which he obviously was.

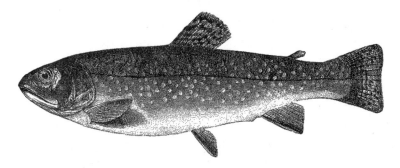

Even in court, Przybyla continued to claim that he had not had a single beer that evening, and that his blood alcohol level was so high due to the fact that he had eaten beer battered fish. The jurors found his explanation a little fishy and concluded that he was guilty of his tenth offense of operating a vehicle while intoxicated.

## YOU CAN'T MAKE A HORSE DRINK, BUT YOU CAN MAKE IT TAKE YOU HOME

Louisiana cowboy Jack Williams was almost charged with a DWI when he was pulled over along Highway 16 near Baton Rouge, but was only given a ticket because he was riding his horse.

Williams had been towing some horses around with his truck that day when he decided to stop in a local bar for some daiquiris. After putting a few down and visiting the restroom, it was time for him to hit the road home. Williams realized how inebriated he had become from the deceivingly sweet yet strong drinks, stumbling into the parking lot towards his truck and trailer full of horses.

Williams is an upright guy with good values, and he knew he was in no condition to be driving himself and his horses back to the ranch. So he decided to saddle up his favorite horse.

A little worried about the cowboy and his horse, Sugar, on the side of a busy highway, a deputy stopped the two to make sure they were okay, soon realizing Williams had had a little too much to drink. Although they couldn't charge him with a DWI, he was still cited for public intoxication. He later reported that it was the safest option for him to get home because the horse still knew the way when he didn't.

## TWO DRUNKS WITH ONE STONE

A Vermont trooper was able to bust two drunk drivers in one stop on Interstate 91 outside of Rockingham. The two men were stopped for speeding but were then busted for numerous other offenses.

According to reports, the trooper clocked the car going at 106 mph down the interstate. During the stop, the trooper took the driver, Erik Polite, out of the car to be detained while the passenger, Leeshawn Baker, jumped into the driver seat and put the car in gear. Unfortunately for Baker, it was not the "go-forward" gear but reverse, which sent the car careening backwards toward the trooper's car with the trooper and Polite in it.

The trooper was able to execute an evasive maneuver to avoid the collision, clearing the path for Polite's car to cut across three lanes of traffic and then crash into the interstate median. We're not sure if Baker was trying to get away, but one thing is for sure, he didn't.

The officer now had reason to detain Baker as well and threw him in the back of the car with his buddy, Polite. Breathalyzer tests indicated that Polite was feeling pretty good with a .19 blood alcohol level, while Baker was feeling really good with a .25 blood alcohol level—both high enough for them to receive DUIs.

The charges didn't stop there. After searching their persons and the car, the trooper found ten grams of cocaine, seventy-nine Oxycodone pills, fifty Percocet pills, and a decent amount of marijuana. Needless to say, Baker and Polite were in a little more trouble than they would have been with just a speeding ticket.

## UPROOTED AND SMASHED

This story might take the cake for most totally unaware driver ever. A Chicago-area woman wasn't pulled over for swerving in between lanes, running stop signs, or speeding, but because of a glaring anomaly the officer had spotted: the fifteen-foot tree sticking straight up from the hood of the woman's car.

The fifty-four-year-old, Maryann Christy, was pulled over on January 23, 2016 when the officer spotted her and her tree-stand of a car driving down Spruce Court in the Chicago suburb of Schaumburg. Police had received a report of a vehicle driving with a tree embedded in its grill, but it was hard to believe until it was seen.

Deputy Chief Roman Tarchala pulled Christy over when the strange reports materialized before his eyes. Obviously though, the tree in the woman's car was not the biggest problem. Christy admitted that she had run into the tree, but she couldn't remember exactly where the incident had occurred. Maybe the alcohol had something to do with Christy's forgotten adventure. She was charged with several offenses off the bat, including two counts of DUI, operating an uninsured vehicle, and driving with an obstructed windshield.

After scanning the area to find where the accident had occurred, the Schaumburg Police located the site where the tree had been hit, separated, and inserted into the grill of Christy's car—nearly five miles away from where she had been pulled over.  On top of her DUI charges, she was also charged with failure to report property damage and damage to village property.

## MEDICAL PROBLEMS LEAD TO A LOSS OF CONTROL

You can be distracted from the road by any number of things: your phone, people pulled over by the cops on the side of the road, horrific crashes, chatty passengers, or your favorite song coming on the radio. But one thing that will divert all of your attention from the road while you're driving is a medical emergency. A driver of a Ford Mustang in Woodhull Township, Michigan, lost complete control of his car when he suffered from a medical problem while on the road. The loss of control led the car to stop at a place where you would normally never see a car: the roof of a house.

Woodhull resident and eighty-three-year-old Joyce Kingsley heard a loud crashing noise one day as she was futzing around the house. She thought it was the weather picking up for a storm but there wasn't a cloud in the sky. Upon looking up, she noticed that a new Ford Mustang was on top of her roof.

The driver of the Mustang suffered from a medical problem while driving on Interstate 69 and lost control of his car. The Mustang veered off of the interstate, crashed through several sets of bushes, trees, and a fence and then came to a stop onto the roof of Kingsley's house.

Kingsley's house is butted up against a hill on its backside where the roof is nearly level with the ground, providing a perfect driveway for the car to make it onto her roof. The roof was not badly damaged and the driver of the car was not hurt, although he was taken to the hospital for low blood sugar. Kingsley plans to put a tarp over the damage until it can be fixed and also wants to put up guardrails around the backside of her property.

# CHAPTER 4:
# EXTREME SHOPPERS AND EXTREME CONSUMERS

There are extremes in all walks of life. From athleticism to ideologies, people are able to push the limits of almost everything they participate in. People have lived and died for all of the extreme walks of life, including shopping. There are no limits in how you can shop and consume. You can be extremely frugal and save yourself mass amounts of money on the things you need, or you can be extremely excessive and spend mass amounts of money on things you will never use. It's all a matter of your situation and how that situation dictates your spending habits. Some are in the position to spend and some are not, but the extremes that people go to while they spend are equal on both sides of the board.

People can save millions and they can waste millions, but most will do whatever they can to take advantage of the best deals and the best products. How far are people willing to go? Well, some are willing to spend millions of dollars in a matter of hours while others are willing to only spend tens of dollars on toilet paper in three years. Both are extreme representations on how far people are willing to go with their money. Some think their money can give them whatever they want, while others rely on other methods to fulfill those desires.

Where have these spending habits come from? For some on the frugal extreme, these habits come out of necessity from their tight budgets as living wages go down and cost-of-living goes up. For some on the excessive extreme, these habits may come from a life of opulence. Shopping is a prerequisite to existence in this day and age. People must work and exchange their labor for money in which they can buy the products they need to survive. There are very few things in this world that you need that can be acquired without this exchange of goods, services, and capital. The limits in which people can spend are determined by their situation, but the extremes of low- and high-cost spending are rare examples of how people can take this necessary pastime too far.

## BLACK FRIDAY AND AGGRESSIVE SHOPPERS

*You know exactly where "thankfulness" has gone when the new major event of Thanksgiving is Black Friday. The day when thankfulness should be at the top of our minds is now filled with thoughts of the hottest deals and the newest products. There is no being thankful when the wish to have more and more preoccupies your mind. All Americans have heard the horror stories of Black Friday stampedes, injuries, and in-store fistfights. Shoppers waiting in anticipation outside of stores have crescendoed into consumer riots that need local police forces to tame them.*

*Not only do people fist fight, but they trample employees and fellow shoppers; they pull out guns in defense of their right to a specific deal; they scheme against each other; and they prepare their list for months and wait outside of stores for weeks. There is no other shopping extreme that can compare to the consumer frenzy that is Black Friday. People must be awfully thankful to be able to acquire the products that lay outside of their economic reach during every other time of the year.*

## HOW MUCH, REALLY, IS THAT DEAL WORTH?

One woman was so desperate for a discounted video game console that she sprayed her fellow shoppers with pepper spray. The incident happened in 2011 at a Walmart in the Porter Ranch area of Los Angeles, California.

Firefighters treated ten people who were exposed to the spray at the scene, and no one required hospitalization.

The woman sprayed the crowd as people were grabbing for Xbox video game consoles. But according to Officer Robert Chavira, a police spokesman, the suspect was actually able to sneak away from the crowd, pay for her purchases, and leave the store before police arrived.

A witness who was looking at a Wii video game, Juan Castro, said he and other customers were hunting for "deals," when the woman began spraying shoppers.

"I don't know if she felt threatened or she felt she had to do that to get what she wanted," Castro told reporters. "I didn't see her personally, but I sure got the scent of the mace. I got it in my throat. It was burning. I saw people around me, they got it really bad," Castro said.

"I tried to get away as quickly as possible because I didn't think it was worth it. No deal's worth that," he said.

## LOCALS CAN'T BE THANKFUL WHEN THERE IS SO MUCH MORE TO HAVE

In 2009, Black Friday shoppers in Upland, California, caused such a disturbance that the local Walmart was forced to shut down for more than two hours.

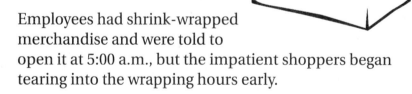

Store management called Upland police at 2:44 a.m., asking for assistance in dealing with customers who were "fighting inside," said Lt. Jim Etchason.

Employees had shrink-wrapped merchandise and were told to open it at 5:00 a.m., but the impatient shoppers began tearing into the wrapping hours early.

"This was without a doubt the worst I've ever seen it," said one veteran employee. "They wouldn't let people line up," she added. "They were belligerent. They just bombarded the store."

Police arrived on the scene as store managers kicked everyone out of the store, Etchason said. The bargain hunters were told to line up in the parking lot.

While the customers were outside, their carts were emptied and all items were returned to the shelves. But even with the police presence, people began yelling and screaming, pounding on the glass doors, and attempting to sneak back into the store through the lawn and garden section.

Eventually, store managers were able to calm the crowd, and when police officers left at 6:15 a.m., "everyone was behaving themselves," Etchason said. The store reopened a bit before 6:00 a.m., and allowed customers to reenter in groups of thirty. By 9:00 a.m., it was a normal Black Friday again, with packed shopping carts and long checkout lines.

## MAN CLAIMS THE DEALS ARE HIS MUSE

A veteran Black Friday shopper in Arizona has been first in line at his favorite Best Buy every year since 2007. Jarvis Johnson lives in his decked-out tent for a week, awaiting the store opening and writing raps to pass the time.

Until the store opens, at 5:00 p.m. Thanksgiving night, Johnson hangs out in his campsite, which includes a TV and a microwave.

"The early bird gets the worm," he told reporters, "And I'm the early, early, early bird so I got the worms."

Johnson's camp has gotten more elaborate every year, he said. In 2015, for instance, his Best Buy campsite included a big-screen TV, a twin-sized bed, a cooler filled with food, and a microwave.

And while he waits for the doors to open, the freestyle rapper kills time by writing rhymes about all the deals he's hoping to get.

"I hope you like the price, 'cause they very, very nice. I'm doing what I do, I'm trying to get a TV just for you. $149 for a forty-nine-inch, I hope you like TV 'cause I like it, too," he rapped during a TV interview.

Experts said that more than 135 million shoppers hit up Black Friday sales online and in stores in 2015.

## A SHOPPER'S GUIDE TO SELF-DEFENSE

An armed shopper who pulled out a handgun during a 2012 Black Friday scuffle at South Park Mall in San Antonio, Texas, was within his rights, according to police.

An hour after the store opened for Black Friday shoppers, police were dispatched to the Sears in the mall after receiving a call about a shooting, according to an incident report. When they arrived, they detained Jose Alonzo Salame, thirty-three, who was holding a black 9-mm semi-automatic handgun.

"We don't see this very often," Officer Matthew Porter said, adding that Salame did not break the law by displaying the weapon. "He was within his rights."

Salame had a concealed handgun license, and he told officers that he pulled the gun out to defend himself after he was punched in the face by Alejandro Alex, thirty-five, who had tried to cut in line. Salame said he feared further injury by Alex, so he held the gun as a deterrent.

Some witnesses reportedly had a different story, telling police that Salame had provoked the situation by behaving rudely, and then pulling the handgun out and pointing it at Alex. But San Antonio Police Sgt. Rob Carey said that Salame had actually pointed it at the ground.

A witness at the Sears store, Roger Rivera, said Salame was punched and then pulled a gun. Customers immediately ran, "tumbling over things, dropping boxes," Rivera said.

After the situation was resolved, Salame was released from police custody and he and his family were asked to leave the store. The report states that a manager gave him a store voucher.

"We're glad the incident was resolved peacefully," said Sears spokeswoman Kim Freely. "The safety of our customers and associates are our No. 1 priority."

## A NEW TREND IN SHOPPING

*Mobile technology has changed the shape of many things in the world today. You can talk to anyone from across the world; you can receive emails in nature preserves; and you can look up information at any whim of your inquisitive mind. Access to communication, entertainment, and information is now constantly at the fingertips of millions of people throughout the world.*

*As opposed to the super computers of yesteryear that took up the space of multiple rooms, personal computers have continued to downsize from fitting on our desktop to our pockets. We can fulfill our careers with these devices as well as spend our money. They replace many tools of the past with one efficient machine that connects us with the world. How people shop has been changed forever with online stores and mobile technology, and now, shopping with your mobile device will transform once again with a relatively simple product.*

## APPLICATION KEEPS STORE OPEN AT ALL TIMES

Imagine using an app to enter your grocery store and to purchase everything you need. An entrepreneur in Sweden has created just such a thing.

"Stealing from this shop is more stupid than stealing from an ordinary shop," says Robert Ilijason, a thirty-nine-year-old IT consultant. Ilijason created Näraffär—a small grocery shop in the southern Swedish village of Viken, about an hour north of Malmö. To enter the store, he swipes his smartphone to unlock the door.

The first thing a shopper will notice about Näraffär is that it has no staff and it never closes. In order to start shopping, you need the app to get in and to make purchases. Ilijason, who lives in the small town of Viken, created the app in early 2016. One evening, he dropped the last jar of baby food in his house, and discovered that all the shops in his town were closed. He had to drive to another town before he found an open grocery store.

Although the app has created much interest, Ilijason laughs it off. "The solution is not original," he says. "I'm using off-the-shelf products and have added very little." Despite his modesty, Näraffär —which roughly translates to "the shop nearby"—could signal the beginning of a new way of shopping.

At the moment, Ilijason is still testing both the app's functionality and features. His goal is to eventually launch shops like Näraffär in other small towns. "I want to learn that the technology works and then improve the concept, so that any small town can apply it," he explains.

To start shopping at Näraffär, customers download the app, which is linked to their bank account (they receive a monthly bill). Ilijason runs a credit check on all applicants before they can begin using the app. Once approved, customers can use the app to unlock the door and start scanning products with their smartphones.

Even with no staff in the shop, theft is highly unlikely. Ilijason has set up security cameras in the store which capture every move. If he notices a discrepancy when he does weekly inventory, he can look at the security footage and see who was in the shop when the item went missing.

Some experts think his app—or one like it—has much potential. And "smarter" versions of the app could succeed, too. For instance, an app that recommends items based on your shopping history, or one that notifies you if you've forgotten something on your list. Still, Ilijason retains his humble modesty over the buzz his idea is getting. "It's easy to over-think it," he says. "But it's just a shop."

# COUPONING AND FRUGAL SPENDING

*Although price of living has gone up over the past few decades, there are still many ways in which you can finagle a bargain and save some major cash. Couponing has a history dating back to the 19th century in Atlanta, Georgia, with the stupendously successful Coca-Cola Company. Used as a marketing scheme to increase sales of their product, coupons have provided a viable path for people to save money on everyday products. You can buy massive amounts of toilet paper for half the cost. You can receive a rebate on a portion of the money you originally spent on an item. You can get a range of products for a discount without having to do anything more than to remember to bring your coupons with you.*

*Some may think it's a sign of poverty when people use coupons, but on the contrary, people have been able to come out of poverty with the use of coupons. As you save money on products, you can spend the excess cash on paying off debt or other large expenses that are looming over your head. But sometimes couponing goes a little too far. People collect stockpiles of products they've bought with coupons throughout their house, although the products won't be used for years and years. There is a fine line between using coupons to be frugal and using coupons in excess. Either way the etreme shoppers use their coupons, couponing is most definitely an extreme case of frugality.*

## FAMILY LIVES THE HIGH LIFE, FRUGALLY

Jordan Page from Draper, Utah, is known as the "Queen of Frugal." The young mother of four was forced to change her lifestyle after a housing project she was working on with her unemployed entrepreneurial husband, Bubba, fell through.

The pair was hit with $15,000 in credit card debt and little income. So Jordan made changes anywhere she could. She stocked up on coupons, bought cheap drugstore makeup, started doing her own hair instead of visiting pricy salons, and even took leftovers from neighbors to supplement her food budget.

Now, years later, the stay-at-home mother and her family are clear of debt, and Jordan has started a blog and YouTube channel to help people with their own money-saving issues.

In one of her YouTube videos, Jordan demonstrates how to style hair without going to the salon, and expounds her love of $0.99 eyeliner.

"I'm a busy mom, I don't have time for complicated makeup! This is my no-fail routine that I use every day . . . and it uses mostly drugstore products!" she tells viewers.

On her blog, *Fun Cheap or Free*, Jordan says it's essential to make financial plans for the year ahead, like plotting out birthdays and anniversaries in advance to save for gifts. Vacations take extra planning, as well, she says, so cheaper accommodations and flights can be researched.

Even though their finances have improved, Jordan and her husband—who now runs a tech start-up—continue living their frugal lifestyle.

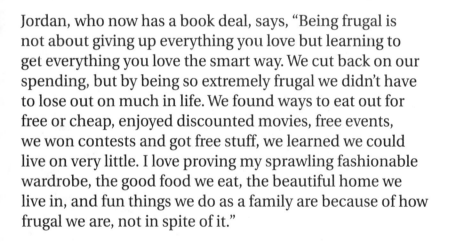

One of the purchases they're proudest of is their $1 million house, which they bought for only $400,000. And in an effort to further reduce the house price, they even sold the basement to Jordan's parents to use as a vacation home.

Jordan, who now has a book deal, says, "Being frugal is not about giving up everything you love but learning to get everything you love the smart way. We cut back on our spending, but by being so extremely frugal we didn't have to lose out on much in life. We found ways to eat out for free or cheap, enjoyed discounted movies, free events, we won contests and got free stuff, we learned we could live on very little. I love proving my sprawling fashionable wardrobe, the good food we eat, the beautiful home we live in, and fun things we do as a family are because of how frugal we are, not in spite of it."

Jordan realizes that many people look at her "cheap" lifestyle with distaste, but it doesn't bother her.

She said: "The greatest compliment is when I go to a business event or a blogging conference and people ask if I'm a fashion blogger. When I reply 'no, I'm a frugal living blogger' the stunned look on their face is priceless."

## PINCHING PENNIES PASSED
## DOWN THROUGH THE GENERATIONS

When Karen Hoxmeier's parents divorced when she was a teenager, she quickly learned the value of bargain shopping. With four kids to support, her mother struggled to provide everything she and her siblings needed. And extras, like new clothing, were rare.

"Anything we wanted we had to find a way to get a good deal on or we weren't getting it," she recalls. "That's when I discovered clearance racks."

Hoxmeier, now a stay-at-home mom of three, writes a blog to help others who need to save money. *My Bargain Buddy* is a site that promises you'll "never pay full price again."

"I don't pay full price for anything," says Hoxmeier. And that includes everything from Coach bags to swimsuits to movie tickets.

When it comes to groceries, Hoxmeier always lets her area stores dictate her family's menus each week. Before shopping, she looks through each store's specials and buys according to what's cheapest. If a store is having a sale on chicken, for instance, her family will have chicken dinners that week. And when she finds an especially good deal on freezer items, she buys in bulk and loads up the freezer in her garage.

Hoxmeier is now passing along her clearance rack shopping skills to her two teenage daughters.

She gives them a budget and allows them to buy what they want. "I think giving them a budget and putting them in control makes them more responsible," she says. And the teenagers have quickly learned that their money can either go to a single full-price item or several sale items.

During a recent trip to Kohl's, Hoxmeier gave her daughters $30 in coupons and gave them free rein in the store. To her surprise, they followed their mom's advice and came back with armloads of clothing from the clearance rack.

## SIMPLE DEBT RELIEF: WORK HARDER, SPEND LESS

Extreme couponing goes beyond regular old bargain shopping. Just ask Nathan Engels, who is known as "Mr. Coupon."

"People that just sort of haphazardly clip their coupons and stroll through the aisle, they're going to save a little, but they're not going to make a huge difference at the bottom line of their grocery budget," says Engels.

Engels runs a blog called *We Use Coupons,* named after the response that he gives when people ask him how he saves so much money.

The twenty-eight-year-old from Villa Hills, Kentucky, often spends no money at all on groceries, thanks to his extreme couponing skills. His garage is filled with stockpiles of items like toilet paper and frozen vegetables.

"The last time I purchased toilet paper at the store was in 2007," he says, adding that a three-year supply only cost him $30.

Like many other extreme couponers, Engels started clipping coupons as a way to get out of debt. He and his wife are now debt-free.

"When my wife and I got married in 2007 we started to look at our finances and we realized we had $17,000 in credit card debt alone. We said, 'We need to do something different. We need to start saving, we need to pick up more hours at work.' So what we did is we started to do everything. We worked harder and we started to look at coupons," Engels said.

## MAN UNMATCHED AT PRICE MATCHING

Like many retailers, Kohl's department store promises to price match if you find a better deal at another store. But according to shopper Israel Mata, there are limits to the store's generosity. In fact, Mata says he was blacklisted from Kohl's website for price matching too much.

Mata never had a problem with ordering from Kohl's, and frequently made use of the store's price match policy. But recently, his shopping hit a snag.

"My order kept getting canceled," Mata said.

Acccording to Mata, Kohl's was advertising a chest of drawers for $1,200 online, but he found the same chest on another website for just $109. On top of that,

Kohl's was offering an extra twenty percent on a total purchase. The discounts brought the price down to just $79 per chest, so Mata ordered six of them. But the store canceled three of the orders.

And then they went one step further. "They told me due to the fact that I price matched so much that they decided to ban me and freeze my account," Mata said.

Paul Ivanovsky writes about Walmart deals on his blog, *I Heart the Mart*. He says that consumers should go ahead and take advantage of retailers' generosity, but should also be careful about going too far. Stores can always stop customers from cashing in on big deals.

"They almost always give their mangers the authority to say, 'nuh-uh' on an item,'" Ivanovsky said.

The moral of the story: although many places price match, most reserve the right to cancel a deal. And always follow the rules to avoid complications.

## LOCALS STRICKEN WITH MATERIALISTIC OBSESSION

A new crop of savvy shoppers has popped up in online communities. Shoppers often buy in bulk, and fill empty corners of their houses with extra boxes, bags, cans, and containers of everything from potato chips to shampoo.

While it may seem like these people are stocking up for a hurricane, extreme couponers are a growing flock of consumers looking for the best bargains.

The shopping devotees have created online communities, where they trade tips and information through Twitter and Facebook, or on blogs like *Slick Deals* and *The Krazy Coupon Lady*. Together, they hunt out digital, mobile-phone, and paper coupons, which they use to buy their large hauls of merchandise.

Sometimes, extreme couponers are even able to find such good deals, they end up getting stuff free of charge. Online message boards are filled with shoppers who brag about stockpiling groceries and then selling them for a profit at garage and yard sales.

## COUPONERS CONTRIBUTE TO COMMUNITIES IN NEED

Single mom Tina Klein used the lessons she learned from her extreme couponing skills to start the Super Coupon Woman Foundation. The foundation has donated thousands of dollars in food, clothes, and toys to her community.

Klein came up with the idea for her foundation after going through a divorce and struggling to make ends meet. When friends, family, and even strangers offered to help her, she knew that one day she would repay their kindness by paying it forward to others in need.

"Even though I didn't ask for it, random strangers would step up to the plate and help me with whatever I needed," she explained. "I wanted to give back to my community to do what others did for me."

Inspired by "Coupon Mom" Stephanie Nelson, an extreme couponer, Klein began using her own frugal skills to buy products cheaply and donate them to different organizations. "Once I made my very first donation and saw how it could help other people, it inspired me to keep going and reach higher amounts," she said.

Klein set small goals for herself at first, donating $200 in goods for which she only paid $50. But then she continued to challenge herself with larger goals, until she was finally able to donate $100,000 with the help of extreme couponers around the country.

"Together we can make a difference, cutting hunger one coupon at a time," she said.

## TEENAGER COLLECTS COUPONS FOR CHARITY

Jordon Cox, of Essex, England, was only sixteen years old when he turned an extreme couponing talent into a holiday gift. Even though his own family was struggling, Cox decided to make sure other families had enough to eat during the holiday season.

The thrifty young man—who only paid about $0.16 on his family's plentiful Christmas dinner last year—was able to purchase three grocery carts full of food for the hungry, the *Telegraph* reported.

Cox collected 470 coupons throughout the month of December in order to buy the food. The total came to about $935, but once those hundreds of coupons were factored in, the final tally was a mere $0.07.

Cox donated the food to Doorstep, a charity that disperses food to disadvantaged families.

"The Christmas shop was definitely the best experience of my life," Cox told the *Telegraph*. "I feel so pleased that I could help so many people."

Cox's passion for coupons began after his parents got divorced and he watched his mom, Debbie, struggle to make ends meet.

"Before my mum and dad split up I didn't have a care in the world for what I spent," he told the *Mail*. "But now mum has to support both of us and it's quite hard. I just want to help her any way I can and I found the best way to do that was through couponing."

Cox has made a name for himself in the coupon world. He has been invited to speak at conferences and lectures as far away as Orlando, Florida, and gives out tips on Facebook and Twitter. He hopes to launch his own website soon.

## COUPON SCHEMES SIMILAR TO DRUG CARTELS

Phoenix police arrested forty-year-old Robin Ramirez, forty-two-year-old Amiko Fountain, and fifty-four-year-old Marilyn Johnson after the trio took extreme couponing too far. The three were running a counterfeit coupon scheme, the *Associated Press* reported. Police recovered $40 million dollars of fake coupons from the women's homes, according to a local TV station.

*Yahoo Finance* reported that up to forty major manufacturers, including Proctor & Gamble, were affected by the illegal operation. The manufacturers joined the Phoenix Police Department and the FBI to investigate and ultimately stop the illegal ring.

The fake coupons were allegedly sold through sites that eventually helped coordinate the investigation.

Police also seized $2 million in assets from the three homes, which included vehicles worth $240,000, 22 guns, and a 40-foot speed boat, according to reports. Sgt. David Lake of the Phoenix Police Department described the women's lavish lifestyles as the "equivalent of drug cartel-type stuff," according to reports.

The three suspects were charged with illegal control of an enterprise, forgery, counterfeiting, fraudulent schemes, and artifices and trafficking in stolen property.

# THE SHOPPING SPREES DREAMS ARE MADE OF

*Aside from all of the other extremes, nothing seems to wow the people more than stories of multi-millionaires spending their millions in ridiculous ways. Excessive shopping seems to take the idea of shopping a little too far. With people spending millions of dollars in one day, there is no way one person can utilize everything that was bought with their fortune. Millions of dollars can provide basic living wages for many people, but instead it's spent by one person of extreme wealth.*

*Is charity dead? Do we not give away our money to those in need anymore? Do we only give our money to corporations and companies who look out for nothing other than the bottom line? There isn't much hope found in these stories of excessive spending. But maybe you can start dreaming of how you can spend millions of dollars on those around you who are in need.*

## THE OUTER LIMITS OF SPENDING

One of the most famous examples of an extreme shopper has to be Imelda Marcos, wife of Philippines dictator Ferdinand Marcos. The two fled the Philippines in 1986, but not before Imelda amassed her famous collection of about three thousand pairs of shoes.

But shoes are not all the first lady bought. On a trip to New York, Rome, and Copenhagen in 1983, Imelda spent $7 million in ninety days. On just one of those days in New York, she spent $3 million. Her purchases included

$2 million in fine jewelry and $35,000 on limousines. In Rome, she purchased a $3.5 million Michelangelo painting. Her extravagant travel expenses are the stuff of legends: she once spent $2,000 just for chewing gum during a stop at the San Francisco airport. Another time, on a plane departing Rome, Imelda realized she'd forgotten to buy cheese and forced the pilot to do a U-turn in mid-air.

In 1981, Sotheby's abruptly canceled a $5 million art auction because Imelda wanted to purchase every item in the catalog before the sale even began. And when single items weren't enough, she began purchasing entire buildings in her favorite shopping capitals, including the Woolworth Building in New York. She even spent $10.3 million to renovate an entire town in the Philippines when one of her daughters got married.

Imelda spent five years in exile, and returned to the Philippines in 1991. Her assets are still being contested; in 2012, the *AFP* reported that Imelda's declared net worth was $22 million.

## ATHLETICISM INCREASES AS SPORT SHOPPING BECOMES OFFICIAL

Is shopping a sport? According to San Francisco State University professors Kathleen O'Donnell, associate dean of the School of Business, and Judi Strebel, chair of the marketing department, for some people it can be. The two recently published research online about "sport shoppers."

"This is somebody who takes great pride in their ability to get the thing they want at a discount," O'Donnell said. "It's not about spending the least, it's about saving the most."

O'Donnell is the lead author on an article in the *Journal of Retailing and Consumer Services*, with Strebel and their Australian colleague Gary Mortimer of Queensland University as co-authors. The article, titled, "The thrill of victory: Women and sport shopping," was published online in November 2015.

According to O'Donnell and Strebel, a "sport shopper" can often afford to buy items at full price, but still looks for a bargain just for the thrill of it. In a sense, they see it as a competition, and a way to outsmart the retail system. And just like actual athletes, sport shoppers can recall many of their achievements, like how much they paid for purchases, or the dates they got the best deals.

And the similarities don't stop there. Sport shoppers and athletes also create strategies to achieve their goals. Just like a runner trains for a race by building up endurance and mapping the race's route, a sport shopper will study details like store layouts and merchandising patterns.

O'Donnell says the difference between a "sport" shopper and a "bargain" shopper is that a bargain shopper generally looks for the best deals out of necessity, whereas a sport shopper just likes the "rush" of finding a deal.

O'Donnell thinks that her research could benefit the marketing efforts of retailers.

## PRINCESS WITH A BAD SPENDING HABIT

Plenty of hoteliers have stories about guests attempting to sneak out without paying the bill. But most of those guests aren't Saudi Arabian royalty. On May 31, 2012, Princess Maha bint Mohammed bin Ahmad al-Sudairi attempted to leave Paris's five-star Shangri-La Hotel, where she and her entourage of sixty people had been staying for five months. Unfortunately, she failed to pay her $7 million bill first. It took many calls to high-ranking officials and diplomats before the matter of payment was finally worked out.

Apparently Princess Maha assumed she could slip out of the hotel unnoticed. After all, according to press accounts, she almost got away with $20 million in merchandise in Paris three years earlier. In that case, the princess didn't even attempt to pay, but rather had an assistant hand the shop merchant an officially embossed document that said, "Payment to follow." Most of us could never get away with handing over an I.O.U. in place of cash—even a fancy, embossed I.O.U.

And while the princess did, at one time, make good on her promises to pay merchants, eventually, the checks stopped. "She was a very good customer for eight years, but then simply stopped paying," said the proprietor of the lingerie store O Caprices de Lili. Maha owed nearly $100,000 to the shop. One shop owner reportedly even spent days in the lobby of a hotel where the princess was staying, in an attempt to procure payment. Eventually, the vendor filed a civil claim against Maha, but some reports say that all of the princess's debts were eventually settled by the Saudi Embassy.

And the princess doesn't only frequent high-end shops. "She shopped everywhere, from Hermès to Zara and anywhere in between," an acquaintance says. In fact, Mara once owed $125,000 to a discount shop called Key Largo, located in a mall near the Trocadéro in Paris. The shop sells mundane items like sneakers, underwear, and jeans.

According to the acquaintance, during one shopping excursion in Geneva, Princess Maha bought enough merchandise to fill four trucks. She even bought a Lamborghini and a Ferrari, despite the fact that women are not permitted to drive Saudi Arabia.

But perhaps even stranger is the fact that many of Princess Maha's purchases are never even used. "There were rooms and rooms full of bags and boxes," says the acquaintance. "Everywhere you looked there were boxes and bags, almost all unopened."

# CHAPTER 5:
# EXTREME APPETITES AND STRANGE DIETS

Your gastroenterologist may be a little sickened by the contents of this chapter, but when it comes to the weird and strange things locals throughout the world do, diets and eating habits take the prize. From strange cravings to excessive eating, people have yet to find a limit to what, how, and how much they can eat. People love food. They identify their regional cultures with the dishes they prepare: sacred ceremonies are surrounded by the festivities of feasting, and familial traditions are hinged on cooking techniques passed from one generation to the next. But no matter the comfort and peace you feel in eating a traditional meal you grew up with, there are always anomalies that will break your conventions.

Some people may eat too much of a specific food, while others may eat too much of objects that aren't considered food. Food makes us who we are. You consume and replenish yourself; you fill yourself with life giving energy that keeps your body operating as it should.  But sometimes, people take it too far. There are diseases that create cravings for metal, clay, and a whole assortment of "non-edible" objects that people hide from their loved ones for many years. There are cultures that one-up others with the strange menu items that cannot be found anywhere else. There are new techniques in cooking with the burgeoning high-culture of gastronomy where chemistry, biology, and the culinary arts converge in the kitchen of the most expensive restaurants on Earth.

There are no true limits of how or what you can eat. You can adapt and adjust your palette and push the limits of what you might consider palatable. These days, you can eat live octopus, a Cessna 150, your own hair, or anything really—no matter how unhealthy it is. Doctors are solving more and more strange digestive problems everyday, so go ahead and try to confound them with your strange diet.

## PICA IS NO JOKE

*Pica is an eating disorder that many people try to grapple with. Its name comes from the Latin word for magpie, which is a bird found throughout the world that is known for its ability to eat almost anything. Pica doesn't lessen your appetite or stop you from eating altogether, but—because of a mineral deficiency in the body—causes its victims to crave unsuitable and unusual food sources. People with an iron deficiency may develop pica by starting to crave metal, nibbling on tiny pieces of broken metal to satiate themselves and their indescribable urge. There are dozen of subtypes of pica like trichophagia—the urge to eat fiber or hair—xylophagia—the urge to eat wood—coniophagia—the urge to eat dust—and many other subtypes that lead people to eat very disgusting things that we will not dive into today.*

*You may be asking yourself, "But you can't have a hair or wood deficiency in your body, so why should pica also cause people to eat these objects?" That's a great question, with not a very good answer. Pica is mysterious. Many scientists believe that obsessive-compulsive disorder and schizophrenia can also be a cause of the disorder, making it more of a psychological condition than a physical one. Other causes may be linked to sensory, sociopsychological, or cultural attributes in a person that lead to the syndrome. Either way, pica may seem strange or repulsive to some, but it is a serious condition that leads many people to the hospital due to digestive complications.*

## NO JOKE: MAN EATS WHOLE AIRPLANE AND LIKES IT

Michel Lotito was a French entertainer better known as "Monsieur Mangetout"—which translates to "Mr. Eats All." As you can guess, Lotito got the nickname because of his habit of eating just about anything—bicycles, television sets, beds, and even an entire Cessna 150 airplane. Throughout his life, it is estimated that Mr. Eats All ate around nine tons of metal!

It is said that Lotito suffered from pica, a condition that causes cravings for non-food items like dirt, chalk, and glass. In Lotito's case, it also caused cravings for metal. The disorder can be dangerous, leading to blocked intestines, lead poisoning, and other emergencies.

But doctors determined that Lotito had an extra-thick lining in his stomach and intestines, making it possible for him to eat inedible objects without as much of a risk for internal damage. He was even known to eat substances that would've been poisonous to most people.

Before he ate, Lotito would drink large amounts of mineral oil in order to help guide the foreign material through his digestive system. He would then break the objects into small pieces, and drink plenty of water while he ate.

He limited his metal intake to about one kilogram per day, so it could take a while for him to finish a "meal." It took him an entire two years to consume the Cessna, and bicycles took several sittings. Strangely, while Lotito seemed to have no trouble with metal objects, he had a hard time digesting bananas and hard-boiled eggs!

Lotito died at the age of fifty-seven. His official cause of death was "natural causes." But one must wonder if his bizarre eating habits contributed in some way.

### MAN KEEPS POCKET
### CHANGE IN HIS PAUNCH

In 2002, a sixty-year-old man went to the emergency room in Cholet General Hospital in France. He had been suffering from a painful, swollen stomach, and doctors were startled when they realized why. The man had eaten about three hundred fifty coins as well as various necklaces and needles.

The man's family told the doctors that they knew of his penchant for swallowing currency, and tried to keep both coins and jewelry away from him. He would even steal coins and eat them when visiting friends' houses.

But even though doctors were warned of the man's issue, they were amazed by the twelve-pound mass they discovered when they x-rayed the man's stomach. It was so heavy that his stomach was forced out of place and sat between his hip bones.

According to one of his doctors, intensive care specialist Dr. Bruno Francois, the patient had swallowed the coins—both French currency and later euros—for over a decade.

## WOMAN'S COMFORT FOOD IS THE FOAM FROM COUCH CUSHIONS

When Adele Edwards' parents were going through a divorce, the then ten-year-old needed a way to cope. So she turned to a rather strange source of comfort: eating foam couch cushions.

Over the last twenty-one years, the Florida mother of five has continued to eat the foam inside cushions. In one year alone, she ate through seven sofas. Edwards even stuffs pieces of foam into her purse when she leaves the house so she can snack on the substance all day.

According to her doctors, her habit is very dangerous and could cause a fatal stomach blockage. Edwards has already had a foam blockage the size of a grapefruit that forced her to take large amounts of laxatives. When she recently also began ingesting dirt, her doctor diagnosed her with iron deficiency. Edwards now takes iron supplements and is trying therapy and hypnosis to cut down on her appetite for foam.

## NEW YORK WOMAN LOVES BABY POWDER

Since she was thirty years old, Donna Lee, a fifty-two-year-old woman from Queens, New York, has eaten baby powder. Although she can't remember ever craving the substance before then, an aunt says that she used to reach for the powdery stuff even as a baby.

Lee considers baby powder a "snack," and likes to eat a handful after breakfast every day. She also keeps a bottle on her nightstand so she can snack on it while she's lying in bed. According to Lee, ingesting the powder gives her a feeling of comfort and satisfaction.

Embarrassed about her habit, Lee didn't tell anyone about it until recently. Since pica sufferers are often deficient in vitamins or minerals, such as iron, Lee was placed on a vitamin regimen, and since then, her unusual appetite for baby powder has decreased.

## MAN WANTS TO OUTSHINE HIS PEERS AND BE THE SUBJECT OF A TOAST

A stand-up comedian from Wooster, Ohio, says he enjoys eating things like champagne glasses and lightbulbs because they make him feel "warm and tingly."

The man, who was featured on the TLC show, "My Strange Addiction," is known only as Josh. He says that eating glass is like chewing "sharp rock candy," and although there isn't much of a taste, he likes the gritty texture.

Josh started eating glass in 2007, and by the time the show aired, he had eaten around two hundred fifty light bulbs and one hundred glasses. When his fiancé first heard of his glass-obsession, she assumed it was part of his stand-up routine. But Josh insists that eating glass has nothing to do with comedy.

According to him, he first started eating glass because he read about it in a book. He was hesitant at first, but once he realized he had no ill-effects, he kept going.

Mostly, though, Josh eats glass because he loves the attention he gets at parties and when he's around friends. When he's alone, he usually sticks to more traditional fare, like actual food.

## ODD CASE OF HAIRBALLS

In 2007, the *New England Journal of Medicine* reported on a strange case. An unnamed eighteen-year-old went to her doctor with pain in her abdomen and an unexplained forty-pound weight loss. She had been suffering for five months, and doctors used a small camera to look inside the woman's stomach.

What they found was rather surprising. A huge hairball was lodged in her stomach, filling almost the entire space. That's when the patient revealed that she had a habit of eating her own hair, a condition called trichophagia. Doctors performed surgery to remove the tangled mass, which turned out to weigh a whopping ten pounds!

After five days of recovery, the woman left the hospital with instructions to follow up with a psychiatrist. Happily, within a year she had regained much of her weight and had managed to break her dangerous hair-eating habit.

## WOMAN EATS NEWSPAPERS WHILE PREGNANT

A pregnant woman from Dundee, England, can't help but keeping herself up to date with the newspapers. Not that she's reading them, she's just making sure she keeps the day's paper on her just in case she gets a food craving. The thirty-five-year-old Miss Curan has developed a strange taste for the flavor of newspapers during her latest pregnancy with her fourth child.

The strange thing is that the cravings for her first three children were normal, but for this fourth child she cannot control the hankering she has for the hot-off-the-presses news. And it's not just any paper that she'll eat. She has tried a lot of them but has a strong preference for the *Evening Telegraph*. Curan says, "If you shredded up lots of different papers, I would know exactly which one was the *Evening Telegraph*."

Her cravings have taken her so far that she even anticipates the weekends when the papers aren't printed and stocks up on Fridays to make sure she has paper to eat. Her children do not understand her habit and have tried it themselves, thinking the taste was absolutely horrible. Although her family might not be so supportive, her friends keep their papers around for her to collect when she needs them.

# THE STRANGE DELICACIES OF GASTRONOMES

*High culture and sophisticated societies of people often intrigue those who lie outside of those distinct social circles with their curated and refined manner and tastes, their food, and their culture. The practices of those in the cultural elite often go way outside of their comfort zones to try the most exotic and privileged food in the world. There is no living creature too strange to be consumed for those who can pay for it.*

*Gastronomes are the enthusiasts of the food world, collaborating with regions, traditions, cooking practices, and good manners to create dining experiences that fulfill not only your senses but also your intellect. There is nothing like sitting in a pre-fixe restaurant, analyzing a fine bottle of Côtes du Rhône with your nose, and having fifteen of the most meticulously crafted and well thought out courses of food brought to your table by a server. Well, there are a lot of things that could beat that, but nothing can beat the sense of entitlement you will feel under said situation.*

*Eating is truly a culture in and of itself that is of the essence of every one of us. We all have our own culture of eating.*

*We like what we like; we don't like what we don't like. Everyone is brought up under certain traditions that surround food. While you may stay within the boundaries of those culinary traditions, with a globalizing world, there are opportunities to try food outside of your personal culinary cultures that will expand your perception and shrink your wallet.*

## ECCENTRIC FARE TAKES OFF IN CHICAGO

If you're the kind of person who likes to play with your food, perhaps you should visit Alinea in Chicago, Illinois. The three-star Michelin restaurant recently began serving an unusual dessert—the Edible Helium Balloon.

Head chef and Aliena co-owner Grant Achatz is the mastermind behind the dessert, which is being hailed as one of the most innovative in the country. He recently released a video to show how the balloon is made, which starts by whipping up a green apple taffy base. The taffy is then connected to a tube and blown up with helium. The "balloon" is then tied off with a string of dehydrated granny smith apple, and sprinkled with a dusting of green sugar.

Diners are given the option of either popping the balloon with a pin, or sucking out the helium. Most diners opt for the helium, as the high-pitched helium voices provide extra entertainment as they consume their dessert.

Achatz is considered one of the best chefs in the world, and Alinea is one of only twelve Michelin three-star restaurants in the U.S.

## DEADLY DELICACY

In Japan and Korea, there is a delicacy known as *odori don*. But to eat it, you have to be a fan of really fresh seafood. *Odori don* is a live squid or octopus, served on a plate while it's still moving.

To be fair, chefs remove the brain before it is placed on the plate, so it's not technically alive. But since it certainly was, moments earlier, still swimming, it continues to thrash around even as you pour soy sauce over it. Supposedly, this is because the creature's nerves and muscles are still active and spring to life when they come into contact with salt. But this seems to be little comfort for people who prefer their food to be inanimate.

Fans of the dish say the writhing tentacles are part of the appeal, but it should be noted that eating *odori don* can be dangerous. The suction cups from the octopus' tentacles can attach to the inside of your throat, choking you. In fact, the delicacy is considered so unsafe that it's banned in many countries.

## COLD DRINKS ARE UNACCEPTABLE IN CHINA

Americans enjoy glasses of ice water quite frequently, especially on hot summer days. But to the Chinese, our cold-water drinking habits seems strange—they much prefer their water to be piping hot.

"In the big family I was brought up in, no one would dare to pour even room temperature water," journalist Nicole Liu writes for the *LA Times*. "Doing so would risk a chorus of criticism, with parents, aunts, cousins, and grandparents chastising you almost simultaneously: 'Cold water gives you cramps!'"

According to Liu, China's love of hot water began in 1949, when the quality of tap water wasn't very good. The government suggested boiling it to kill bacteria. "There were boiler rooms in every workplace and community, and people delivered hot water to each household," sixty-eight-year-old Li Zhenhui told Liu. "They would do it very early in the morning by filling the containers you left outside the door. They kept saying it was for our health and hygiene."

Chinese medicine has long held the belief that hot drinks are more beneficial than cold. Consuming warm water is said to aid digestion, improve circulation, and relieve sore muscles. Whereas cold water was believed to cause cramps and slow organ function.

Some Chinese people find it difficult to adjust to the cooler drinks served in other parts of the world, so hotels and airlines are starting to tweak their services. "Hotels overseas are getting hip to Chinese tourists' needs," Liu says, "adding amenities like slippers, Chinese-language newspapers, and—yes—teakettles."

## INSECTS ARE THE PROTEIN OF THE FUTURE

An artisanal pasta maker in France has created a product that is flying off the shelves. The secret ingredient? Insects!

Stephanie Richard was looking for a way to create a high-protein pasta for athletes, so she decided to try adding insects to her pasta on a whim. She began creating pasta using "insect flour" by pulverizing crickets and grasshoppers and adding them to the pasta. Surprisingly, the pasta was a huge hit and Richard has had trouble keeping up with the orders.

Richard uses a mix of around seven percent insect flour and ninety-three percent spelt wheat flour, and occasionally she'll add ground mushrooms for extra flavor. The end result is a brownish pasta that tastes "like whole wheat pasta," she says.

Richard is now hoping to expand her shop to keep up with the demand for her pasta.

"The insect is the protein of the future," she says. "It's protein of high quality that is well digested by the body." And a 2013 report by the UN Food and Agriculture Organization agrees, saying that insects have "huge potential for feeding both people and livestock."

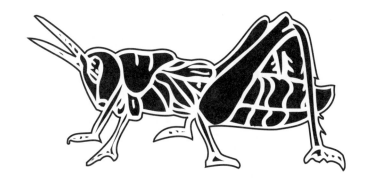

## FORAGING KEEPS MAN'S DIGESTION FROM FALTERING

If you suffered with chronic stomach issues, how far would you go to cure yourself? A man in southeast China uses a rather startling remedy: he eats frogs and rats!

Yang Dingcai claims that forty years of swallowing live tree frogs and rats has kept his digestive system running smoothly. While it seems like a rather unpleasant and extreme measure, Yang has passed his wisdom along to others who claim it works.

One of his devotees is sixty-six-year-old Jiang Musheng, who has suffered from frequent abdominal pains and coughing since the age of twenty-six. But one day, he met Yang Dingcai, who suggested the tree frogs as a remedy, according to the *Beijing News*.

"At first, Jiang Musheng did not dare to eat a live, wriggling frog, but after seeing Yang Dingcai swallow one, he ate . . . two without a thought," the paper said. "After a month of eating live frogs, his stomach pains and coughing were completely gone."

According to the paper, Jiang has also added live mice and baby rats to his unusual diet.

### THE TRUE PRICE OF FARM-TO-TABLE DINING

While making and eating a sandwich isn't extreme, spending $1,500 and six months to make it certainly is. That's what Andy George, host of the YouTube series *How to Make Everything*, decided to do, in an effort to show people exactly what goes into making a single sandwich.

George grew and prepared every ingredient for his sandwich and then shared a time-lapse video titled "How to Make a $1,500 Sandwich in Only Six Months" on his YouTube channel. He wanted to help people understand that we take many things for granted, even when it comes to simple things like sandwiches. George grew all his own vegetables, baked bread, and killed a chicken to show that food doesn't magically appear in supermarkets.

George even made his own salt, travelling to the ocean to collect water and boiling it until the sea salt remained. He then used the salt to make pickles, using cucumbers from his garden. He learned to milk a cow so he could make cheese, he harvested wheat, and he collected honey from a beehive to bake a loaf of bread.

Finally, after six months of hard work, it was time to assemble his sandwich. And how does a $1,500 sandwich taste? "It's not bad," he said.

### IS IT REALLY WORTH THE EXPERIENCE?

Chinju-ya restaurant in Japan is definitely a place only the most adventurous eaters would enjoy. And it may even cause a few of them to run away in horror. After all, this is a place that serves things like cooked crocodile feet, grilled piranha, and deep-fried whole salamander.

Chef Fukuoka, who has helmed the restaurant for six years, takes pride in procuring the rarest and most unusual meats from across the world. He has served everything from axolotls (a Mexican salamander) and isopods (a type of small crustacean) to black scorpions and camel meat.

For a Christmas special one year, Chef Fukuoka prepared reindeer steak and minced meat of badger served in a dry curry. Other dishes have included a whole cockroach platter, soft boiled boar foot, whole piranhas, and bear meat stewed with chicken eggs.

And while dessert is usually a course that everyone can enjoy, at Chinju-ya you might want to skip it. For instance, the "contaminated pudding" arrives to your table infested with worms.

Amazingly, Chinju-ya is a popular restaurant among tourists and locals. And while the prices are quite high—the deep-fried salamander is $190—patrons don't seem to mind paying for the experience.

## THE BLACK EGGS OF JAPAN

Owakudani, near Hakone, Japan, is a large volcanic caldera that formed 3,000 years ago when Mount Hakone erupted. The area is still quite geologically active, with boiling pools of water, steam vents, and fumes of sulphur dioxide and hydrogen sulphide. Yet tourists visit the inhospitable spot each year to partake in a Japanese delicacy: black boiled eggs known as *kuro-tamago*.

The eggs have a startling black appearance, but they're simply regular old chicken eggs. The black color comes from being boiled in the hot water pools of Owakudani. The sulphur in the water reacts with the eggs' shells, turning them black and giving the eggs a sulphur-tinged smell and taste.

According to legend, eating the black eggs will prolong a person's life by seven years. The eggs are cooked in large batches in the waters of a spring on top of a hill, where they're loaded onto large metal crates and lowered into the spring water, which reaches temperatures of about one hundred seventy-five degrees fahrenheit, for an hour. They are then steamed at over two hundred degrees for fifteen minutes. When they're done, the shells are black, but the insides are still white and yellow like a regular boiled egg.

Visitors to the boiling site are served the eggs at a shack with small wooden tables, with a magnificent view of Mt. Fuji.

## TOO MUCH TO HANDLE

*In our age of consumption, having an excess of resources may be a sign of opulence, but—as they say—too much of anything is not good for you. Even natural goods can be the demise of the healthiest person around. Gluttony was viewed as a taboo for much of the history of western culture, but it isn't necessarily a taboo that is all that often eschewed these days. Humanity once thought it was gluttonous to consume in excess because it was wasteful and diverts victuals from those who were in need and hungry, but today people have a different mindset as to what is deemed for them over what is deemed for others. People look out for themselves, but sometimes egocentrism has its downfalls as well.*

*People relentlessly give themselves what they want over what they need, and sometimes what they need is much less than what they want. They let their desires take control of their habits, leading them on a path of impotent, lethargic, and gluttonous ways. Sometimes you can eat too much in one sitting and sometimes you can eat too much of one thing over time, but either way, the effects will catch up with you. Take some notes on the following people as they lead themselves down the path of gluttony and try to avoid their practices.*

## NEW KING IS CROWNED WITH SIX WHOPPERS A DAY

Dale Shaw of Duncansville, South Carolina, experienced a wake up call about his diet as weight and heart complications arose. Shaw was known to eat six Whoppers from Burger King a day, along with three servings of large fries and three diet cokes. Shaw felt good for his age and didn't think his diet would ever catch up to him. He ran and lifted weights, but that wasn't enough to keep up with his diet of 8,000 calories and 300 grams of fat a day.

It wasn't a breakfast, lunch, dinner type of schedule, but a lunch, dinner, and late-night snack type of schedule. He was always on the run as he and his wife were raising their three boys and working full time—turning to fast food for a meal became the quick and consistent option they chose to eat a lot of.

Although Shaw felt relatively good, he had his first angioplasty (a procedure that widens clogged or obstructed arteries or veins) at the age of thirty-nine. Shaw's doctor now claims that there is no such thing as too young for heart disease, and Shaw is a perfect example of people not taking care of themselves. Although Shaw has not had a heart attack yet at the age of fifty-seven, he's had recurrent problems with clogged arteries.

Shaw now admits that he really didn't change his eating habits until nearly ten years after his first operation, and he now regrets not taking better care of himself. Shaw really took control of his diet when doctors implanted five stents in the span of two days in 2006. He now enjoys lightly sautéed vegetables over a Whopper meal, but he still gets cravings that he needs his wife to talk him away from. Doctors say that you can exercise all you want, but you can't eat six Whoppers a day and expect to be healthy. It doesn't work that way.

## GLUTTONY KILLS THE KING

King Adolf Frederick was the king of Sweden from 1751 until his death in 1771. On February 12, 1771, apparently the king was extremely hungry. He indulged in a feast with enough food to feed a whole dining room full of people. Reportedly, he ate lobster, caviar, sauerkraut, and herring, and washed it all down with champagne.

And for dessert, the king had one of his favorite sweets: semlor. Semlor is a Swedish cream puff filled with marzipan and topped with whipped cream. While it sounds delicious, the king ate an astounding fourteen servings of the pastry, served in hot milk.

Perhaps unsurprisingly, King Adolf Frederick died later that day, apparently of digestion problems.

## COUPLE TAKES THEIR HASH BROWNS SERIOUSLY

A couple in Mesa, Arizona, took their McDonald's breakfast very seriously, and wouldn't leave without their hash browns. They confronted employees and even called the cops in order to get their fair share of fried potatoes.

The couple ordered two breakfast meals one morning as they were driving around on the bright Arizona morning when things took a turn for the worse after they didn't receive their hash browns. The meal comes with hash browns, so Nova Shaw went inside to try to get what they had ordered. Her husband, Michael Shaw stayed in the back parking lot of the restaurant to call the cops before he went inside to talk to the manager.

After employees reportedly refused to give the Shaws their hash browns, Nova sent the food back their way, throwing the carry-out bags across the counter at the employees. She later said, "And that was out of frustration which I probably shouldn't have done, but I did. Fighting over $2.00 of hash browns is ridiculous. It is ridiculous to have to fight that hard just to get customer service." We're not sure if the employees of the restaurant completely refused to give them hash browns, or if they were just overwhelmed with the aggressiveness of the couple.

Michael went inside after he called the cops and went behind the counter to confront the manager about getting some hash browns on the house. The manager tried to explain that the problem could have happened because the store was still new and the employees were still under training, but nothing was good enough.

The customers' aggression led several of the employees and other customers to call 911 as well. Eventually, the authorities arrived and cited the Shaws with assault and disorderly conduct for throwing their food at the employees.

## MAN ADVISED TO TAKE IT EASY ON THE CARROTS

Who knew that carrots could kill? In 1974, Basil Brown was a fitness fanatic and health food advocate in England who decided to start drinking copious amounts of carrot juice.

According to reports, Brown was drinking a gallon of carrot juice a day, and also taking vitamin A supplements. According to an article in the *Ottawa Citizen*, a doctor advised him against taking the supplements because of his enlarged liver, but he ignored the advice.

After ten days of drinking the carrot juice, Brown died

of cirrhosis of the liver. While many stories blame the overabundance of carrot juice for his death, experts believe the more likely cause was an overdose of vitamin A supplements.

Either way, Brown's story is an example of the danger of too much of a good thing.

## NOTHING BUT POTATOES

Tired of his binge eating habits, an Australian man has decided to adopt a different sort of extreme diet. Andrew Taylor is attempting to eat nothing but potatoes for an entire year.

Taylor, who weighed around three hundred thirty pounds before embarking on the diet, says that the potato diet helped him lose about twenty pounds in the first month alone.

"I wanted to change the way I thought about food so that it's not controlling my life," he said. "When you've got an addiction, a drug addiction or an alcohol addiction, the best thing you can do is stop taking drugs or stop taking alcohol. You can't do that with food. So I thought, what else can I do? Perhaps I can choose one kind of food."

Taylor says that potatoes get a bad rap in the nutrition world, but aren't the food villains some think. "People in the past have had nothing but potatoes," he explained. "People tend to think of them as empty calories. I'm hoping to show that potatoes are a health food."

Taylor claims that since he started his diet, he gets ninety-nine percent of his calories solely from potatoes. He includes sweet potatoes for variety, and sometimes cooks them with  milk, but never adds oil or butter.

Eating only potatoes has helped Taylor break past eating habits. "I've changed from seeing food as a way of getting comfort or pleasure," he says. "I've been exercising more, I'm full of energy."

Nutritionists aren't convinced that Taylor's plan is sustainable, and say that he can't get all of the nutrients he needs just from potatoes. And even Taylor himself says that he doesn't recommend that anyone follow his diet.

## THE INTERNATIONAL CONNOISSEUR OF MCDONALD'S

For most of us, McDonald's is a place we stop at when we're in a hurry and don't have time for anything else. But for Canadian software engineer James McGowan, the fast-food chain is a bit of an obsession. McGowan has traveled to fifty-three different countries just to sample the regional dishes found in each country's McDonald's restaurants. He writes about his travels on his blog, *Traveling McD's*.

McGowan has sampled foods like a creme brulee McFlurry in Singapore, salmon burger and teriyaki rice in Thailand, tofu nuggets in Japan, churros in South Korea, and poutine in Montreal.

McGowan reviews all of the foods he tries, and not all of it is to his liking. The lychee pie in Kuala Lumpur, for instance, got a zero-star rating. "The flavor was far more acidic than a pie filling should be, and just didn't go well with the fried crust at all," he wrote. He also wasn't a fan of the "disgusting" tuna pie in Thailand, "chewy" homestyle chips in Copenhagen, or the thick and syrupy bubblegum McFizz in Singapore.

But McGowan has plenty of favorites, too, like the matcha McFlurry in Singapore and a cheese panini in Tahiti.

McGowan hopes to soon visit McDonalds's restaurants in Oman, Mongolia, Qatar, and Vietnam. "Strangers say, if you're fortunate enough to go to all these countries, why do you waste it on McDonald's?" he told the *Wall Street Journal* "I like sharing online. People seem to enjoy it."

Plus, he adds, "I don't drink. I don't smoke. This is my vice."

## MAN LOVES CHIPOTLE A LITTLE TOO MUCH

Mark Rantal, from Colorado Springs, Colorado, really loves Chipotle.

In 2015, Rantal ate at the restaurant every single day for more than one hundred days. He says his habit started by accident. "On Monday I decided to get Chipotle and on Tuesday I made the same decision, then got lunch with my friend there on Wednesday," Rantal told reporters. "We laughed about it at lunch and he asked how long I thought I could go. And that began the thought."

After going every day for a week, Rantal kept going every day for a month, and then just kept continuing because it was "very easy."

"Every time I hit a milestone it was very easy and convenient to imagine hitting the next. Plus, it's a little ridiculous."

Even though Chipotle has hundreds of different possible combinations of rice, vegetables, beans, and salsas, Rantal orders the same thing every time: a burrito bowl with white rice, pinto beans, fajitas, sofritas, mild salsa, corn, medium salsa, cheese, and lettuce.

"For me food is one of those things I look at as fuel instead of celebration. I've just never really gotten so into it," he told reporters. "It became so convenient if you know where you're going, you know the friendly faces of the staff, you know you enjoy the meal, and you know you're going to get the calories."

Rantal says he was given about one of every ten of his meals on the house. He also admitted that after one hundred days of Chipotle, he gained about fourteen pounds!

## BIG OL' BURRITO CHALLENGE

A video online has debuted an upcoming competitor in the competitive-eating world. Kate Ovens devoured a mega-sized burrito and gained a spot on the wall of fame at Zapatista's in the UK. The famed burrito of the Belly Buster Burrito Challenge at the restaurant challenged Ovens, but Ovens had no problem meeting the challenge and devouring it.

The burrito is filled with chicken, pulled pork, rice, beans, and sour cream and looks to be nearly two feet long. Ovens had no problem eating the massive burrito. Her total time from end to end was eight minutes and twelve seconds, which is under the competition's limit of ten minutes. Ovens didn't even seem to struggle to eat the whole thing. She provided commentary throughout her meal and even joked around a bit with her big sombrero on.

Female competitors are now coming out of the woodwork to throw the competitive-eating world for a loop. A New Zealand pageant winner and model, Nela Zisser, has also been completing gastronomic feats that astound many of her viewers. Zisser saw Ovens' video and challenged her to a McDonald's challenge. Ovens declined because she admits that she is nowhere near Zisser's eating level yet.

# CHAPTER 6:
# WEIRD COLLECTORS AND THEIR ODD COLLECTIONS

Everyone has that one activity or interest that gives them their identity. Some may be interested in playing music and identify themselves as musicians, while some may like to write and read lines of verse and so consider themselves poets. Your activities can give you a sense of purpose and an area of esoteric knowledge in which you can inform others about. Everyone takes pride in their interests and looks for others to share them with—even if their interests are a little off kilter from what may be considered normal.

Collectors are a special bunch of people. Their collecting interest might have been sparked as a child or they might have emerged by the time they were an adult, but either way, the objects they collect are a part of who they are and who they identify themselves as. Although collectors may have many people to relate to about collecting, there may only be a few people in the world that will find their toenail-clippings collection interesting. Collectors can always relate to other collectors about collecting, but their collections may be a little too specific for others to enjoy.

Collecting is a strange mix of financial devotion, obsession, and materialism that culminates into an activity that may not be the healthiest or rewarding activity one can participate in. Large collections can overrun the collector's house, leaving little room to actually be lived in. Collections can even be a health hazard if they are not managed and stored properly. Collectors might have a preference for vintage items that are no longer in production or they can have a general collection that focuses on a broad theme in which to include more items. A collector can be awfully specific in what they are looking for if they are trying to complete a series or a set of items, or they can be very inclusive as to what can join the ranks of their collection.

There is no limit to what you can collect. With the industrial revolution, massive amounts of products with endless variations from different companies and years provide a never-ending supply of things to add to collections. You can collect Coca-Cola brand merchandise or Disney memorabilia and there will never be an end to variations you can find. Or you can collect esoteric items that will take years of searching and antique shopping to find. It doesn't matter what you collect, but just make sure your collection is large enough to impress people before you start telling them about your odd obsession.

## WORLD RECORD COLLECTIONS

*Children often dream about breaking a world record when they get older. They dream of breaking the record for the highest base jump or the record for fastest speed achieved in a car, but not necessarily the world record for largest collection of umbrella covers. Sometimes collections of things can be awesome and sometimes they can seem a little ridiculous, but at least they give hope to those childhood dreams of breaking and holding a world record. Collecting may not take as much skill or training needed to break an extreme world record, but it can definitely take its toll on the life of the collector.*

*Breaking the world record for the largest collection of anything can create a large dent on the collector's budget and can even negatively affect their social life. Collectors spend large amounts of money to attain new pieces for their collection and go to even further lengths to find the one piece that is missing from their collection. Collecting is close to an obsession. Collectors' identities of themselves are intricately wrapped up in their collection, seeing it as a vital part of who they are and what their interests are.*

*It takes a specific type of person to want to collect a rare cultural artifact, and it takes a whole different person to go as far as breaking the world record with their collection. Some record holders even had to convince the world record authorities that their collection is worthy of being considered a legitimate collection to be recorded. Who knew that toenails and miniature chairs are collected to such great lengths? Who knew that people would want to collect traffic cones from around the world? Collections can get awfully strange awfully quick, but the collections are nowhere near as strange as the collectors themselves.*

## THE OHIO TROLL COLLECTION

Cuyahoga Falls, Ohio, resident Sherry Groom, a psychiatric nurse for twenty-five years, has 3,254 troll dolls. In 2013, her collection set the world record for the largest collection of trolls according to the World Record Academy.

"I came from the era when people thought collecting things was a cool thing and it just so happened that I had a couple of people who were generous who said 'Oh! I'll get you a collection,'" said Groom.

Groom owns and operates Villa Maria Dementia Care Center in Alliance and she also owns the Troll Hole Folk Art Gallery. The gallery is located near the nonprofit Arts for Alzheimer's Gallery on Main Street where her troll doll collection will be permanently housed.

Groom and her husband, Jay, ultimately plan to turn the gallery into a full-service arts center with studio space, workshops, a 200-seat performing arts center, and art classes geared toward helping dementia sufferers and their caregivers.

## REALLY, THERE'S NOTHING BETTER TO COLLECT?

When most of us buy umbrellas, we probably remove the fabric sleeve and toss it away. But not Nancy Hoffman of Peaks Island, Maine. Hoffman has been carefully preserving, cataloging, and displaying discarded umbrella covers at her Umbrella Cover Museum since 1996.

After working hard for decades to preserve these mundane items, Hoffman was finally recognized with a world record. But first, she had to convince the folks at Guinness World Records to create a category for the most umbrella covers. And in 2012, they finally agreed.

"Despite their mundanity, umbrella covers deserve their own category," said Hoffman. "They are kind of cute and they seem to be purposeful, but to me, the great attraction is the stories. I've got one that a woman found a few years ago at the remains of the Berlin Wall. She had to shoo away two young lovers who were flirting near it," said Hoffman. "I just got one from Italy. I got another one sent to me by a man who runs a toilet paper museum in Amherst, Mass., and he found it at the Amherst landfill."

Hoffman believes her umbrella covers help remind people that even the little things in life have stories worth repeating. Her appreciation is reflected in her museum's mission statement:

"The Umbrella Cover Museum is dedicated to the appreciation of the mundane in everyday life. It is about finding wonder and beauty in the simplest of things, and about knowing that there is always a story behind the cover."

### LARGEST—MASTICATED—GUMBALL

Normally, chewed gum is something to be discarded and never seen again. But for Barry Chappell, it's a collector's item.

Chappell was a heavy smoker for many years, but when his son was born fifteen years ago, he decided to kick the habit. He immediately quit smoking, using Nicorette gum as a way to curb his cravings. But what began as a promise to his family to commit to a healthier lifestyle soon turned into a world record.

It all started on a long flight to Europe in 2006—Chappell had nowhere to throw away the piece of gum he was chewing, so he simply rolled it into a tiny ball and held it in his hand. Throughout the flight, as he chewed more gum, the ball slowly grew, as layer after layer was carefully molded upon the last. By the time the flight landed, wad of gum in hand, Chappell vowed to create the world's largest gumball.

Now, six years and 95,200 pieces of gum later, Barry is a non-smoking superstar. He created a gigantic piece of chewed gum that weighs 175 pounds and measures 62 inches in circumference!

## HUSBAND HAS NO PROBLEM
## WITH WIFE'S COLLECTION

Deb Hoffmann, a computer software designer from Waukesha, Wisconsin, might be the world's biggest Winnie the Pooh fan. To prove it, she's created the world's largest Winnie the Pooh memorabilia collection, landing a place in the *Guinness Book of Records*.

Hoffmann has around nine thousand items—worth as much as $94,000—in a collection so big it fills the four rooms of her four-bedroom house.

"I have been collecting for twenty years," says Hoffmann. "I remember it started with maybe twenty different Winnie the Pooh toys a year, but then it got worse and sometimes I'd be picking things up on a daily basis. I scour thrift shops and websites like eBay for anything to do with Pooh and his famous friends including Tigger, Piglet, and Eeyore.

"I've got the stuffed toys and figurines, bags, mugs, and cereal boxes. I've even got 475 different items of clothes with their faces on."

Even though her collection takes up much of the space in her house, Hoffmann's husband, Craig, is fully supportive of her hobby. Craig, also a software designer, has even created a database so his wife can keep track of what she's bought. He also drives her around the country to collect more Pooh memorabilia.

He says, "There are two rules when it comes to Winnie the Pooh—I get to tease Deb about her collecting, and she can continue as long as I don't get kicked out of bed because she's using the space to store more collectibles."

Deb adds, "Some people think the collection is great but others will ask me why I need so many. I think of it as just a fun thing and it's pretty harmless. I might slow down in the years to come but I don't think I'll ever stop."

## A COLLECTION OF SMALL CHAIRS

Georgia resident Barbara Harper Hartsfield has collected miniature chairs since 1999. In 2006, she founded the

Collectible and Antique Chair Gallery, in Stone Mountain Village, to exhibit her unique collection.

In 2008, the collection was recognized as a world record holder for its 3,000 miniature chairs.

The chairs are constructed from a vast array of different materials and range in size from miniature to doll chair sizes.

The chairs are displayed within twenty-seven major exhibits and fifteen smaller displays in the gallery. Visitors can browse chairs with themes such as Christmas, patriotic, beach, and Coca-Cola.

There are also "functional" chairs designed to be used as clocks, lamps, bookends, and cookie jars, as well as a hundred different chair shaped salt and pepper shakers.

## LOCAL COLLECTS TRAFFIC CONES FROM AROUND THE WORLD

Usually, when we see traffic cones, all we think of is construction and the headache they cause. But for David Morgan of Oxfordshire, England, traffic cones are a fascinating collectible.

Morgan has nearly five hundred cones, and is listed in the *Guinness Book of Records* as the owner of the largest collection of road cones in the world.

But while some may think traffic cones are an unusual thing to collect, it makes sense to Morgan, who works for Oxford Plastic Systems. The company is the world's largest producer of traffic cones. And, while working so closely with his collectibles, Morgan became interested in their design.

"It's really interesting," he says. "There are so many different shapes, sizes, and colors. And the models are always changing."

Morgan began collecting cones in 1986, when his company was involved in a legal dispute with a rival manufacturer. He explains, "A competitor wanted to take us to court because they said we had copied their design." Morgan searched the country for cones to prove that the allegations were false, and his company won the case. Thus began a lifetime of cone collecting.

"I'll find out where the roadwork is and go and look for them," he says. "But the best ones are from more unusual places, like village halls and from undertakers—who always have different ones. Everywhere I go, I collect them, but I always take new ones with me and swap them. I would never pinch one, as they're a safety product. I usually ask the foreman, but people aren't really bothered, and most of the cones I get have been stuck on their own for years— sometimes fifteen years after the roadwork is finished."

The oldest cone in his collection is a 1956 rubber cone from Scotland. His collection also includes cones from around the world, from places as far away as Italy, Corsica, and Malaysia.

And he's always searching for new items to add to his collection. "I am still looking for a rare five-sided cone from Manchester," he says. "I hear about sightings, but by the time I get there, they're gone. It's like looking for Elvis."

## COLLECTING TOENAILS IN THE NAME OF SCIENCE

The record for the largest number of toenail clippings may seem like a ridiculous record, but the science behind it is incredibly important in order to better understand diseases like cancer.

The Atlantic Partnership for Tomorrow's Health, or PATH, is part of the Canadian Partnership for Tomorrow Project, the largest study of its kind ever undertaken in Canada. Led by a group of Dalhousie University researchers, Atlantic PATH is investigating the various factors that contribute to the development of cancer and chronic diseases, including environmental factors, genetics, and lifestyle. The study has recruited thousands of men and women from across Canada.

The 30,000 participants have provided the PATH team with the usual sorts of samples you might see in a study like this, such as body measurements and blood samples. But what's more unusual is that the study participants have also given the team their toenail clippings—tens of thousands of them.

"Toenails are an important part of our research," explains Atlantic PATH's Principal Investigator Dr. Louise Parker, professor in the Departments of Pediatrics and

Medicine, as well as the Canadian Cancer Society Chair in Population Cancer Research.

"By the time you trim the end of your toenails, they've been on your body for about six-to-nine months and during that time they're exposed to everything that you're exposed to. What we're particularly interested in, in this context, is the extent to which environmental exposure affects our risk of disease."

Dr. Parker and her team didn't set out to break a record, but nevertheless, collecting toenails from 24,999 individuals was enough to earn Atlantic PATH the Guinness World Record of owning the world's largest collection of toenail clippings.

"My colleagues David Thompson and Trevor Dummer had the idea," says Dr. Parker, when asked about how they decided to submit the collection to the Guinness organization.

"It's a heck of a collection: a quarter of a million toenail clippings altogether. So they looked at the Guinness website and while there were other toenail records—for example, the longest toenails—there wasn't a record for the largest collection of clippings. We thought it was a great opportunity to have a bit of fun after everyone's hard work and commitment to the project."

## LOCAL MAN IS OBSESSED WITH TIME

Mark McKinley, of Amherst, Ohio, has the world's largest collection of talking clocks. With nearly a thousand clocks in his home, he finds it best to set them at different times.

"I don't want them all on time because they would drown out each other," he said.

McKinley, a psychology professor who recently retired from Lorain County Community College, likes to set the clocks for different hours so he can enjoy them throughout the day.

With 954 clocks, McKinley owns one of almost every model made, he said. He owns everything from the very first talking clock ever made, manufactured in 1911, to plastic Looney Toons clocks. He keeps a record of each clock in his International Society of Talking Clocks website, which he founded.

McKinley convinced Guinness World Records to include a talking clock category. He meets all the requirements, of course, and received the recognition in 2010, when he had 782 clocks.

His collection began accidentally, he says, when he bought a talking clock for his sight-impaired mother in 1990.

That clock led him to casually look for other talking clocks in stores and at garage sales. After acquiring seventeen clocks in less than two years, he decided he was a collector. And with the advent of internet shopping, his hobby took off.

He is currently writing a book on the psychology of collecting.

## THE SWEETEST COLLECTION AROUND

Do you throw away extra sugar packets? Well, if you were into sucrology, you would collect them. Sugar packets, which come in many different shapes, sizes, and colors, are quite popular among sucrologists.

Officially, Ralf Schröder, of Lower Saxony, Germany, is the proud owner of the largest sugar packet collection in the world. Schröder owns 14,502 packets of sweetener, dating all the way back to the 1950s.

His collection far surpasses that of Kristen Dennis of Chicago, Illinois, who held the previous record in 2012 with a still-impressive 9,500 packets.

Dennis began collecting sugar packets when she was in high school in the late 1990s. She was inspired after hearing about people who collect ketchup packets. But it wasn't until after she graduated from high school that her collection really picked up steam.

"I don't know why, but I typed in 'sugar packets' on eBay and a whole world was opened up to me," Dennis told reporters. "I didn't know other people collected these things, so I started bidding on them, and eventually the collection grew like crazy."

Dennis keeps her collection in twenty-two binders in a closet of her home. Surprisingly, she doesn't even use sugar in her coffee. But perhaps that explains how she has been able to collect so many packets!

## RECORD BREAKER CAN'T BE STOPPED FROM BREAKING RECORDS

Dr. John "Lucky" Meisenheimer, a dermatologist, surgeon, author, and athlete from Orlando, Florida, owns the largest collection of yo-yos in the world. His collection of 4,251 yo-yos earned him a spot in the *Guinness Book of World Records*, and also inspired him to write his own book, *Lucky's Collectors Guide to 20th Century Yo-Yos*. His book is now preserved in the Smithsonian Institution's National Museum of American History. Meisneheimer is the founding board member of the American Yo-Yo Association.

But if collecting yo-yos isn't impressive enough, Meisenheimer has also been featured in Ripley's Believe It Or Not for, inexplicably, swimming a half mile with his foot in his mouth, wrestling a bear, and setting a world record for ear wiggling. He's also a champion swimmer and a Special Olympics swim coach, and has gained a cult following of fellow swimmers who join him for morning swims in Lake Cane in Orlando.

# STRANGE COLLECTIONS AND THEIR COLLECTORS

*Sometimes the collection and the collector are just as strange as the other. Collectors develop their tastes through an innumerable array of influences that lead them to a passion for collecting a certain type of object. A collection can start out of pure chance when you receive a strange gift that encourages you to find other objects like it, or just by pure fascination. It can be a brand name product or just an item that you can't seem to detach your interest from, obsessing over all of the different products and variations you can find matching your collection's theme.*

*It may seem strange to collect anything, but it will only get stranger as you learn about the things that are actually collected. If something exists, then you can almost guarantee that there is someone out there collecting them. The options of what can be collected are limitless and the variations found within those specific collections are almost just as limitless. You can collect objects with different models, years, and manufacturers, and even objects that can only be found in a specific area of the world. There are no limits to what can pique someone's interest. Everyone is different and if one prefers to collect the wax paper wrappers fast-food burgers are served on over antique Tiffany lamps, then so be it. There is no judgment you can place on the collector, because you know deep down that you would start collecting your favorite objects too if you could muster the passion.*

## EMPTY NESTERS FILLING THE CHICKEN COOP

Joann and Cecil Dixon of Elkhart County, Indiana, have such a large collection of chickens that you can spot them before you even walk into their home. Chicken statues, chicken planters, and rooster lights cover the front yard of these avid poultry collectors. Inside their house, they have just about every kind of knickknack, figurine, plate, salt and pepper shaker, dish, and mug that resembles a rooster, hen, chick, or hatching eggs you can imagine.

The couple, who have never owned a real chicken, led a typical Midwestern life before embarking on their hobby. Joann raised their two children, Paula and Michael, and Cecil sold life insurance. But Cecil says the chicken collecting really took off once they were empty nesters. "My wife and I had more time and more disposable income to pursue collecting," Cecil explained.

"It isn't an expensive hobby," Cecil pointed out. "We both have our favorites but it isn't based on cost. I think the most we have ever spent on one chicken was around $150. Joann knows every one in the collection. I will see something in a store and ask her, 'Honey, look at this chicken.' And she'll say. 'We have that one already.'"

And since Joann meticulously washes and dries the thousands of figurines once a year, she should know. Washing the figurines is a delicate job. "You can't use a duster because it might knock them over." Because the Dixons have such a large collection, the figurines are placed close together and if one is knocked over, it's likely to take many more with it. "It is quite a job. But it is a trip down memory lane too, because as you handle them you remember where you were when you bought it—or who bought it for you."

## LOCAL WOMAN NEEDS A LOT OF ERASERS TO FORGET HER MISTAKES

Make a mistake? Well, you're in luck, because Petra Engels, of Germany, owns the largest collection of erasers. She has 19,571 individual erasers from 112 different countries, which she has been collecting since 1981.

Petra started collecting erasers at the age of nine, after visiting a stationery shop. The shop was selling various unusual erasers, and Petra's interest was piqued. When she was a child, friends of her mother used to give her erasers as gifts instead of chocolate. And her parents would bring her erasers from various business trips.

Petra celebrated the twenty-fifth anniversary of her eraser collection in 2012. The vast collection is stored in twenty-two glass showcases and an additional cupboard with twelve drawers.

## THE CLEANEST COLLECTION AROUND

Carol Vaughn, from Birmingham, England, has collected 5,000 bars of soap since 1991 and has no plans of throwing in the towel.

Her hobby has seen her build up the haul from all over the world and from as far away as Australia.

Her collecting started as a way to pass the time while she was caring for her mother, Ivy May, who died in 1991. But since then she hasn't stopped and can't help looking out for a new bar for her collection whenever she can.

Vaughn said she loves finding a new soap she hasn't seen before and likes to find ones that might seem unusual.

"I was given one by a friend that is shaped like a cheesecake; you don't know whether to eat it or use it to have a wash," she said.

She even added another thirteen to the stash while she was on holiday in Morocco celebrating her sixty-fifth birthday.

"Whenever I go out of the door, I think maybe I will pick up another or see one I like. A lot of my friends bring them to me too. I suppose you could say I do get myself in a lather when I see a soap I really like; it's great to add it to the collection."

Adding that she did not know how much her collection was worth, she said: "It would be fun to have the collection valued, but I don't think the Antiques Roadshow are going to be giving me a call any time soon."

## A NICELY COMBED COLLECTION OF HAIR

John Reznikoff owns a collectibles shop in Westport, Connecticut, where he stores interesting and rare items like a copy of the Declaration of Independence and Ernest Hemingway's briefcase typewriter.

But Reznikoff's most prized possession is something much less mundane: a strand of hair from Abraham Lincoln, taken from him on his deathbed. The curly black clumps reside behind glass, looking like something worthless. But the hair reportedly is worth up to $500,000.

Reznikoff has hair strands from numerous historical figures like George Washington, John F. Kennedy, Napoleon, Beethoven, and Chopin, but he keeps quiet about the impressive collection, preferring only to advertise his stamps, autographs, and Americana ephemera in trade catalogs and newspapers.

The hair collection business can be surprisingly popular, and many people see it as a way to bring in dollars. Recently, Reznikoff sold a few strands of George Washington's hair to Topps—the company known for baseball cards—creating a frenzy when Topps hid the hair in three special cards as part of a promotional contest. However, hair isn't always as lucrative as collectors would like it to be. The same month he sold the hair to Topps, Reznikoff sold a wisp of Beethoven's hair to a company that incorporated it into a synthetic diamond and listed it for $1 million on eBay, hoping for a big payday. However, the diamond attracted only sixty-two bids and was finally sold for $202,000.

But Reznikoff isn't in the hair collection business for the money. "I've always been a collector," Reznikoff said. "I really believe it's something genetic. You're either a collector or you're not."

## LOCAL CLAIMS HE'S NOT A FREAKY COLLECTOR, BUT HE IS

Jens Veerbeck bought his first toaster at a flea market fifteen years ago on a trip to San Francisco, California. Now the graphic web designer from Essen, Germany, owns 600 models, including one worth £3,500 from the 1920s.

"I bought an old chrome pop-up toaster from the 1950s and I initially wanted to use it in my kitchen, but it sparked a love affair which goes on to this day," says Veerbeck. "Six weeks later, I was visiting another flea market in Holland and I found a really small, ugly toaster made in what used to be East Germany, and it was the contrast between the two that got me going."

Veerbeck has created an online toaster museum to display his collection, which he stores in a converted loft of his apartment. Last year, tens of thousands of people visited the website to browse through the toasters.

Veerbeck himself likes to visit the site because, as he says, "It means that I can see my toasters all the time."

Surprisingly, collecting toasters can be an expensive hobby. Some of Veerbeck's toasters have cost as much as £1,500. But according to him, they have more than doubled in value.

"These toasters are now probably worth up to £3,500," he said. "But bear in mind the fact that the collectible toaster market goes up and down more times than a popping piece of bread in a toaster."

According to Veerbeck, different countries have differently designed toasters, and he can tell where a toaster was made just by looking at the design. But he admits that his friends think his hobby is a bit strange.

He says, "Some of my friends think that I am crazy to have such a large collection of toasters, but please believe me when I say that I am not some strange freaky collector who goes around collecting toasters."

## SUPER SIZED MCDONALD'S COLLECTION

An eleven-year-old boy from the U.K. sold his impressive collection of memorabilia from fast food chain McDonald's, and is now £8,000 richer!

The huge collection, which included around seven thousand items, belonged to Luke Underwood. Luke convinced his father, Philip, to buy the assortment of toys, posters, and promotional items, dating from 1990 to 1999, from another collector for just £250 when he was seven years old. The rare memorabilia included the only known complete set of the 101 Dalmatians in their original packaging. Approximately ten thousand Happy Meals would have to have been eaten to create the entire collection, which was believed to be the largest of its kind in the U.K.

Bidders from as far away as Germany, America, and Japan bid for parts of the coveted collection in a sale at Unique Auctions in Lincoln, England. The final sale added up to a grand total of £8,130.

Luke said he was sad to see his collection go but was looking forward to finding something new to buy.

"I didn't really want to sell it, but now I'm planning on saving the money so I can buy something else like this and make some more money," he said.

Luke's family decided it was time to sell the collection after the items started taking up too much space in their home.

"It was all over the house—the front room, the kitchen, and the landing," said Philip.

"This was one of the most unique collections ever to go on the market and the response was phenomenal," said Terry Woodcock, owner of the auction house where the sale took place.

### LOCAL MAN OBSESSED WITH BUYING DRESSES FOR HIS WIFE

Paul Brockman, a German-born contractor who lives in Lomita, California, has been collecting dresses for his wife, Margot, for the past fifty-six years. Margot now has 55,000 dresses, all handpicked by her husband.

Brockman was given the first ten dresses for free, when he worked at a seaport in Bremen, Germany. Workers were allowed to choose any of the merchandise they wanted, so Brockman picked out the dresses for his then-girlfriend, Margot.

The pair soon married, and he and Margot shared a love of ballroom dancing in their free time. Brockman wanted his wife to have a new dress to wear every time they danced. And Margot, who never liked shopping, was more than content to let her husband choose the garments. So he began his wife's dress collection, choosing each one himself.

Eventually, Brockman began buying dresses almost daily. Sometimes he would come home from work with thirty different dresses in tow, which he bought at department store sales and yard sales. When his hobby became more of an obsession, he even stopped searching for Margot's correct size and simply bought whatever caught his eye!

Brockman would sometimes spend all the money he had in his pocket on a dress, forcing him to wait until his next payday to acquire another. The most he spent on one dress was $300, and Margot never wore it. In fact, Margot has never worn most of the 55,000 dresses in her closet, but at least she'll never run out of options!

## BAGGISTS AND THEIR BAGS

Perhaps some of the weirdest collections are also the ones most of us never give much thought to, like airsickness bags. People have collected aviation memorabilia since the Wright Brothers, but baggists—those who collect those little paper bags from the airplane seat pocket—are an especially enthusiastic bunch.

Serious collectors, described on the Baggist Hall of Fame website as "those oft-maligned, always misunderstood, but heroic individuals who have taken on themselves the onerous task of preserving the world's bag heritage for future generations," continue collecting their treasures even as airsickness bags are found less frequently on planes nowadays.

And the baggist community, just like any other community of collectors, has its own superstars and celebrities. Take Dutchman Niek Vermeulen, for instance, who, as of 2012, had collected 6,290 sick bags from 200 countries to earn a spot with Guinness World Records. And Steve Silberberg, of Hull, Massachusetts, created the Air Sickness Bag Virtual Museum where visitors can browse through almost three thousand different airsickness bags.

## SOUTHEASTERN OHIO'S BIGGEST ATTRACTION

Southeastern Ohio's Hocking Hills is a stretch of Appalachia renowned for its natural attractions like caves, waterfalls, and state parks. But visitors may not realize that one of its most unique attractions is located indoors: America's largest collection of pencil sharpeners.

Reverend Paul A. Johnson began the collection in the 1980s after he retired, collecting everything from sharpeners embossed with Disney characters to a sharpener that dates all the way back to 1906. After his death in 2011, his widow, Charlotte, moved the collection to the Paul A. Johnson Pencil Sharpener Museum, located in a shed at the Hocking Hills Regional Welcome Center.

The collection contains more than three thousand sharpeners in all shapes and sizes. The modest little museum is one of the most popular attractions in the area, at least for visitors who are less outdoorsy.

# CHAPTER 7:
# LOCALS SEE THINGS THEY CAN'T EXPLAIN

Paranormal experiences come in all shapes and sizes across the world. From the Stink Ape to the Yeti to Bigfoot, variations on a theme are very common as you begin to research what people have reportedly—yet inexplicably—seen. How are you to perceive these claims?

There is no room for anyone to say that what another has experienced with their own subjective perception of reality is false, but there is no room to just blindly believe everything you are told either. If the whole world believed that it had been visited, contacted, or influenced by extraterrestrials, you would hope that there was solid proof to base those beliefs on. But when you unexpectedly experience something wonderful without being able to explain it, sometimes the physical proof is the last thing you need in order to believe the unbelievable.

How can you validate something you saw in the sky as something not of this earth? How can you tell someone that you saw a ghost? All of these types of experiences have been perceived by millions of people without ever being validated by any kind of authority. The people who have experienced the paranormal don't need an authority to tell them what they saw, but those who are skeptics do. If you have experienced something paranormal yourself, it is then that you can begin to understand the unexplained experiences of others.

Is it because of their open minds that millions of people are able to see what many will never see? Or it is because of sheer luck in pointing their camera in the right place at the right time? Who knows? The paranormal contains a plethora of unexplained experiences millions have had throughout the world without a valid explanation.

## SIGHTINGS OF SPECTERS

*Ghost stories are as old as civilization. The perennial phenomenon is deeply attached to our own existential inquiries that have remained unanswered for all time. What does it mean to live? What happens to what you know to be "yourself" after you cease living? Is your conscience your spirit, and is your spirit present without your physical body? Life after death fills people with the hope that one day they can move past the suffering of the physical world and into a realm of peace, but some may never reach that promised peace. Some may find themselves invisibly toiling and wandering the world after they have died, needing to come to terms with what they were unable to come to terms with while living.*

*There are many mediums in which ghosts are experienced through. People themselves can act as mediums, attracting the specters of the world toward them, offering hope to those who are unable to let go of the material world. Cameras catch glimpses of what was not physically there. Meters of all sorts measure variations in electro-magnetic fields. People see objects move without being touched. Ghosts represent everything we cannot know about our own existence. They represent the spiritual realms that humanity has only dreamed to have existed, but the spirit world just may be the world that lies beyond the standard five-perception reality.*

*Locals from all parts of the world have had similar experiences of frightening apparitions in their photographs or chilling encounters with their loved ones who have already passed. You cannot just claim that these experiences are anomalies or technical hiccups because of the pervasive presence they have on our cultural heritage. The myths of yesterday persist as the paranormal experiences of today, speaking to a select few to divulge their otherworldly messages.*

## GIVING UP THE GHOST

When tropical storm Winston struck the Ra area of Fiji, many small coastal villages were devastated by the rising water and strong winds. The village of Nayavutoka saw the death of two of its village residents in the wake of the storm, both of whom the village respectfully buried as they returned to their storm-torn homes.

One of the unfortunate people to lose their lives that day was thirty-two-year-old Pauliasi Naiova, who suffered from a disability that hindered him from walking at a fast pace. He was known throughout the town for his love of food—never turning down an occasion to eat—and his limp left leg, which dragged along as he walked. He was much slower than the rest of the village, which—unfortunately—thwarted him from making it to safety before the tidal surges hit the coast. The returning village found his body on the beach and buried him later that day.

Disasters like this were to be expected when living on the shore of an island in the ocean, and everyday life went back to normal as people repaired their homes and belongings. But—ostensibly—not everything was back to normal. Nayavutoka native Osea Balesavu, who knew and cared for Naiova, began to notice something strange around the village. That night after the storm, the village dogs barked without stopping. Usually, the dogs reserved their barking fits for predators stalking the village, but that night was different. The night after, the barking continued but everyone—being as relaxed as they are living the island life—took no mind of the noise.

Balesavu went to bed that night like any other night, but something woke him from his midnight slumber. The dogs still barking, Balesavu opened his tired eyes to an apparition of his old friend, Naiova. The sight was surreal in its clarity. Balesavu felt a heavy weight on his chest and saw the image of his late friend standing in front of him, whispering for food. Balesavu was not afraid but knew that the apparition of Naiova could not stay. He told the apparition that he must go, that he does not belong here in this world anymore, that he must leave the village alone and go where he must now go. Despite his wishes, the visitations continued.

Throughout the rest of that week, Balesavu continued to see his deceased friend roaming the village and asking for food. Balesavu reacted the same way every time, telling Naiova that he could not stay there. Although the encounters ceased, Balesavu still felt his friend lingering in the evenings as months worth of dinnertimes came and went.

Balesavu felt great pain for how his friend died, wishing that he could have done more to help him when the storm hit, but it all happened so quickly. Balesavu continues to hope that his friend can find where he must go and be in peace when he reaches his destination. Who knows what happens when you die, but you must seek peace in your place and be able to move away from the material sustenance of our transient world and into the unknown. Let us hope that we are not doomed to wander this planet alone and unperceived when we finally give up the ghost.

## GHOST IN THE MACHINE

Sometimes the last thing you want to see is another email in your inbox that you have to respond to, and other times you receive an email that you cannot help but open. Pennsylvania residents Tim Hart and Jimmy McGraw received an email after their cousin's death that they couldn't help themselves from opening.

Jack Froese died at the young age of thirty-two from heart arrhythmia, but somehow his email account stayed active after his passing. Both Hart and McGraw were totally confounded and a little freaked out when they received awfully specific emails from their deceased cousin. About six months after Froese's death, the two cousins received emails that were incredibly pertinent and related to the last conversations they had each had with him.

Hart received an ominous and downright creepy email from his deceased cousin with the subject heading of "I'm watching!" That alone might have been enough to make most of us freak out and run out of the house screaming, but Hart didn't freak out—at least not yet. He opened the email and it read, "Did you hear me? I'm at your house. Clean your attic!!!"

At that point, Hart felt himself pale of all color. Hart's messy attic was the last thing Froese and Hart had talked about, and now—in true ghost fashion—Froese was probably in Hart's attic looking for a cool, clean, and dry place to hang out for a while. Hart responded to the email, but never received a response.

Froese wasn't done with the internet yet. He purportedly sent another email to McGraw about an ankle injury McGraw had received after Froese's death. McGraw did believe that it was his cousin, contacting him in an attempt to stay connected with his family, but couldn't explain how or why.

Froese's mother, Patty, told the two that what they encountered was a gift and that they should appreciate the mystery. Although some people were upset by the possibility of an online prank, both McGraw and Hart remained confident that their cousin continued in this world as an online presence.

## HOUSE ON THE HILL, MAN IN THE WINDOW

Michelle Widwinter recently bought a quaint home for herself and her daughter in England. After it had passed all of its inspections, the officials decided the home was acceptable to be moved into, but Widwinter soon realized they forgot one last test: a séance to determine whether a man who lived in the house during the 1870s was still living there.

Widwinter didn't look into the history of the house before she bought it, but she quickly realized something was afoot one day as she took a photo of the house's front-yard. Just like all of your worst nightmares, Widwinter looked at the photo and saw the face of a man staring back at her from inside the house. Startled, she ran back inside to make sure no one was there—which there wasn't—and then tried to determine what this apparition was.

Like anyone seeking a public opinion, she posted the photo onto Facebook to see if her friends had any logical explanations for the photo. Some claimed it was a reflection of the flowers in front of the window, others claimed she doctored the photo. Widwinter was a logical person, but logic couldn't explain how a man's face appeared in her window. She soon found herself slipping away from the rational self she had known herself to be when other strange occurrences began to happen around the house.

The face in the window made her question her own beliefs, and then waking up to a wall clock smashing onto the floor made her a believer. She denied any claim that she was making all of it up, but continued to have trouble proving what she was experiencing. Unable to come up with an explanation, Widwinter tried to block out the thoughts of her house being haunted, which was incredibly hard to do because of the persistent and strange noises heard behind the walls and flickering lights seen throughout the house.

It turns out that a local historian, Andrew Jones, had a little insight into the house's history and the man that might have been inhabiting it. Jones studied the life of a man by the name of Samuel Kent, who had lived in that house in the 19th century. Turns out that Kent was the original suspect of the Rode Hill House murder of 1860 before his daughter was convicted and imprisoned for the crime. Because of the dark history behind the house, Jones suspects that the spirit of Kent still lurks in the house, trying to come to terms with the murder of his three-year-old son.

## THE GREY LADY KEEPS HER EYE ON HAMPTON COURT FOR THE ROYAL FAMILY

Cameras seem to be the best way to see something that— ostensibly—isn't there. You can take a photo of your friends in front of a bunch of ruins, but when you look

at the photo you find that there is one more person in the
photo that wasn't really there. For decades the famous
Grey Lady of Hampton Court in England has photo-
bombed numerous photos, appearing in her greyish-blue
gown. The recent photo captured by twelve-year-old Holly
Hampsheir is truly terrifying.

Hampsheir took an ordinary photo—or so she thought—
of her cousin as they were touring the Hampton Court,
a palatial, English estate from the 16th century. She took
a few more photos in the same room and continued on
the tour. Little did Hampsheir know, she had caught a
frighteningly vivid image of the Grey Lady standing right
behind her cousin.

As she reviewed her photos the next day, she noticed the
anomaly in this disturbing photo. She compared it to
the other photos she shot in the room but couldn't make
sense of what she was seeing. The Grey Lady appeared
in one photo and was gone in the next. And this is not
your standard out-of-focus photo of a ghost. The Grey
Lady looks as real as Hampsheir's cousin but is dressed
in an elegant greyish-blue dress with long brown hair.
Hampsheir's aunt, Miss Mcgee, was with the girls when
the photos were taken and was absolutely terrified when
she saw them. Since the encounter, McGee and her
daughter haven't slept properly at night, worrying about
what the omen might have meant.

Grey Lady sightings in Hampton Court have occurred
since 1829, apparently after the palace's church was torn
down, disturbing the Grey Lady's tomb. The Grey Lady's
name was Dame Sybil, who died in 1562 after contracting

smallpox while she took care of the sick infant and soon to be monarch, Elizabeth I. Dame Sybil was a servant at Hampton Court under four Tudor monarchs and had also nursed Prince Edward as a child. After her tomb was moved, many strange noises began to occur throughout the palatial estate. A person had once heard the sound of someone working a spinning wheel through the walls, which led to the discovery of an unknown chamber that contained a single spinning wheel in the center of the room.

Hampton Court is filled with history. It has been home to the British monarchy for more than five hundred years and welcomed history's most powerful people. From all of the servants—like Dame Sybil—who had their entire lives wrapped up in the routine of the palace, to Henry VIII who accused Catherine Howard of adultery and dragged her down the halls of the palace: the Hampton Court has many secrets within its walls. The events that have happened and continue to happen within this palatial estate will continue to captivate the fancies, imaginations, and daydreams of millions of people throughout the whole world. The Grey Lady will continue to walk the halls of Hampton Court to make sure everything remains in order.

## A MUSEUM'S SHROUDED MYSTERY

Texas' Fort Worth Museum of Science and Industry began to notice strange occurrences happening throughout the building after they received the traveling *Titanic* exhibit. Security guards had seen things move across the floor seemingly all by themselves, they heard strange whispers down dark hallways, and they watched security monitors and light fixtures flash on and off. They knew something creepy was about but nothing confirmed their fears more than a recent photo posted online.

The photo—taken in the children's section of the museum—is a shot of a young boy playing with a hands-on activity, but in the background is a figure so distorted and absolutely evil looking that the fun the child is having would be nonexistent if he had seen what was behind him. This figure is shrouded and about the same color as what you'd imagine a mummy to be. Standing in the basket of a child-size grocery cart, the figure's lower half seems to taper off thinner and thinner, while its top half is covered in a tattered fabric with its dead-gray hands holding an undefined object.

Many comments on the page doubt the authenticity of the photograph, saying the figure casts a shadow, or that it's standing behind the cart, or that because the photo is lacking a time signature that it could have easily been altered. But the fact alone is that something this creepy, standing in the middle of a children's exhibit, would have never been ignored by children. It's horrifying and the children would have been terrified if they actually saw someone dressed like that. Doubts and rumors continue to fly around the photo, but we think its paranormal assessment is dead on.

## SUNDAY BEST PHOTO-SHOOT

Flooding the internet these days is a plethora of images that captured sight of things not there when the photographer snapped the frame. Some might claim that dust particles catch the light in just the right way to create apparition-like objects in photos, while others claim that photos are doctored with software to create a buzz. Despite the doubts that surround these photos, many of the photographers claim that they have captured the apparitions of ghosts still wandering our material world.

After a nice bike ride with her friends in Berkshire, England, local resident Helen Andrea found something strange in the photo she had taken of Ruscombe Church. Under the beautiful morning light, the photo shows a ghostly-white figure in the doorway. She didn't notice the anomaly until she returned home later that morning, but after seeing it, she couldn't explain what it might have been. The bike ride wasn't a mission to find paranormal activity, but it ended up being spookier than they had intended.

Ruscombe Church is a historical site that was built in the late 12th century, so it has quite a bit of history attached to it. Whatever the story, it's hard to really know what the photo captured. Opinions remain divided on the photo's authenticity, but whatever you may believe, the photo can still send chills down the backs of the most skeptical of people.

## EXTRATERRESTRIAL MYSTERIES

*The most passionate paranormal enthusiasts are those who have experienced strange things in the sky.*

*Unidentified flying objects (UFOs) create a buzz like none other with the tales that surround them. These types of experiences leave observers stunned, mystified, and suddenly not sure of what to believe anymore. Governments and people will always debate whether what was seen was a secret government project, an alien craft, or maybe a mixture of both. People believe that world governments are complicit in covering up what we know about intelligent life or extraterrestrial beings and crafts. Some people take it even further and claim that the government is working with aliens to subject the Earth's population to intergalactic tyranny.*

*There are many things to believe, but there is little evidence of what we can actually know. To some, it may seem ridiculous to claim that aliens contributed to the development of human civilization, and to others it only makes sense in trying to explain the gigantic leaps in biology and technology humanity was able to make during its evolutionary process.*

*Lights flash, large crafts block out the sky and move silently, memories reemerge from nights of strange experiences with foreign beings, but all of it is only hearsay when none of it can be confirmed. We can't tell if people love to lie about unbelievable things or if they've been changed forever by the unbelievable. Take a look in the sky tonight and see for yourself.*

### NEFERTITI REPLACED BY E.T.

The provenance of Egypt's pyramids has been up for debate since their western-world discovery in the 19th century.

Researchers and archaeologists have puzzled over how a people without the use of modern technology could construct such humongous edifices. Maybe it was slave labor with the help of gigantic pulleys and ramps that put the three-ton, limestone blocks in place. Or maybe it was with the help of extraterrestrial beings and their sophisticated crafts that did most of the grunt work. The answers have been lost in time, but new examinations of Tutankhamun's (King Tut) tomb might lead us to rewrite history to include our extraterrestrial friends in the narrative.

The signs of extraterrestrial activity in King Tut's tomb come from reports by a French archeologist's recent radar scan of the tomb. Archeologist Avril Sap now claims that the myths of Queen Nefertiti's tomb being hidden under King Tut's tomb are false, and that something much more foreign lies within the chamber.

Sap is not alone in her claims. Even the Antiquities Ministry of Egypt has confirmed that what was originally thought to be in there is in fact not in there, and that what is in there is some type of extraterrestrial material that resembles a body. Neither the Antiquities Ministry of Egypt or Sap are confirming that they have found an extraterrestrial's body, but they're not discounting it either.

The tomb has long presented deep secrets to those who have studied it, but this only deepens the mystery. The chamber in question was thought to be the tomb of King Tut's supposed predecessor, Nefertiti, but hidden access into the chamber has prevented archeologists from confirming the rumors. Now, with the recent radar scans of the tomb, the rumors have moved even further away from being confirmed. Sap is now scanning the tomb to find entryways into the chamber but none have been found.

The mysteries of ancient Egypt only continue to grow as what we once thought to be true continues to be disproven. Who really knows how or why King Tut was buried with a blade made from a meteorite? Who knows what really lies within the chamber next to King Tut's tomb? All we know so far is that the Antiquities Ministry of Egypt knows about the extraterrestrial material inside the chamber. Whether or not it's a tomb for an alien is still to be uncovered.

## BE CAREFUL WHAT YOU MEDITATE FOR

A forty-seven-year-old Catforth, England, man, known as Zed, meditated on the thoughts of experiencing extraterrestrials so much that he finally received an answer to his cosmic inquisitions. Apparently, Zed had spent the previous nine months meditating to communicate with extraterrestrials. He got what he meditated for one day as he opened his eyes, looking up to see what he claims to have been some type of ship or being for a brief second.

Zed could not differentiate if what he saw was technological, biological, or a mixture of both. As it soared through the sky, Zed was able to take a few hazy photos of the flying entity in the few seconds that he saw it. He had his phone out in order to document anything that might happen to him, but even in being so prepared, he was not ready for what he would see. Zed remains confused as to what happened that day but has strong inclinations telling him that he did see something not of this world.

This may sound like a fantastic once-in-a-lifetime sighting, but it was not the first time Zed had encountered foreign objects darting, floating, or careening through the sky. He claims to have seen pyramidal crafts that burned a vibrant orange color before, but he has never seen anything that blurred the lines between biology and technology like this. Hopefully, Zed will be able to garner some clarity on the situation as he continues to meditate and strive for enlightenment. Open-mindedness, Zed claims, is the only way in which these mysteries will come to reveal themselves. He wants to help skeptics drop their guard and open their minds to the possibilities of what cannot yet be known.

## AUSTRIA'S ATMOSPHERIC ANOMALIES

The southern Austrian state of Styria is pretty familiar with the paranormal and—what some local paranormal experts might call—mysterious atmospheric phenomena. In recent years, there have been dozens of reports about completely amazing and awe striking aerial objects over the Aichfield Basin in southern Austria but no one—even officials—can explain why.

In July of 2014, one of the most witnessed mysterious atmospheric phenomenon took place over the night sky with hundreds of multicolored orbs moving at tremendous speeds. Many observers first believed it to be some type of natural phenomenon because of the objects' multicolored and fluid-like look, but soon rejected that notion as the objects flew in various formations. Not only that, but these high-speed, multicolored orbs—despite their numbers— were silent. Austrians may be used to seeing things in the sky, but this was surely a mysterious atmospheric phenomenon.

Many officials were contacted that evening for answers, but failed to give an adequate explanation even after some saw the phenomena themselves. Local media contacted traffic controllers for a comment about the event, and although they acknowledge they received many reports that night, they could say no more about the situation.

### MESSAGES FROM MARS?

Rumors of life on Mars have been a common trope in 20th century entertainment, but nothing is getting Martian enthusiasts more excited than NASA's *Curiosity* rover that landed on the red planet in 2012. It has been nearly four years since the rover landed to explore, analyze, and collect compounds, rocks, and atmosphere samples on the planet to determine the possibilities of life. But who's to say that Mars isn't already supporting life?

The rover's right-side navigation camera (navcam) captured a bright speck that flared upward toward the sky as the rover worked its way into new Martian territory, known as Kimberly. The web-master for the paranormal news site *UFO Sighting Daily*, Scott C. Waring, has taken great interest in the photo and what it might mean for life on Mars. He speculates that the speck of light could be a signal from Martians that live under the planet's surface, or, he concedes, it could be a data dropout from the video's transmission back to Earth.

The only hiccup in the extraterrestrial hypothesis is that the rover's navcam system works in stereo and the left-side camera did not pick up the flash of light that was shown from the right side. This could be a major indicator that what was seen was just a data dropout, but the news has many enthusiasts watching. Whether or not Martians are sending up flares from their subterranean abodes is unknown, but with the help of enthusiasts, all of the information sent back from the rover will continue to be scrupulously examined and questioned for any signs of life.

## A SPECK OF A SPACECRAFT

There is a list of telltale signs you can use to determine if you have experienced paranormal activity: You get goose-bumps down your neck when you ask if anyone is there; You suddenly realize that you're missing memory from hours out of your day; Your camera suddenly stops working after you've taken a photo. San Diego County resident Ellen Henry experienced this last sign as she took photos one day of a historical barn in her area. What she originally thought was a speck on her LCD screen just might turn out to be a surreptitious flying craft.

Henry works for the Santee Historical Society and was on assignment one day to update the photographs of the historic Edgemoor Barn. She walked around the barn, scoping the best angles. She snapped a few photos here and a few photos there. She had her eye on the sky to make sure she had the best shot with the best light, but as she double-checked one of her photos, she noticed a speck on her screen—in the sky—toward the top of the frame.

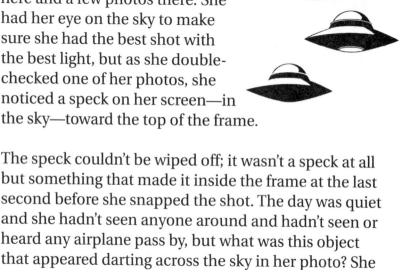

The speck couldn't be wiped off; it wasn't a speck at all but something that made it inside the frame at the last second before she snapped the shot. The day was quiet and she hadn't seen anyone around and hadn't seen or heard any airplane pass by, but what was this object that appeared darting across the sky in her photo? She continued to search for the best angle, but as she went to take another photo, her camera was no longer operating correctly.

After getting home and uploading the photos onto her computer, she soon began to question this little speck in her photo. She zoomed in and what she saw appeared to be an object, silver in color and blurry as if it were travelling at intense speeds. There is no way to tell what the object was, but you can always speculate when things like this happen in such strange situations. Not to mention, Edgemoor Barn has been known by locals to be a hot spot for paranormal activity, including multiple ghost sightings and other mysterious happenings.

## LIGHTS ACROSS TEXAS SKIES

In 1951, reports from hundreds of people in the Lubbock, Texas, area claimed that several sets of lights darted across the night sky at incredible speeds. The sighting occurred in August of that year and was originally reported and confirmed by Dr. W.I. Robinson, Dr. Oberg, and Professor Ducker of the Texas Technological College. As the three gathered in Dr. W.I. Robinson's backyard, they all saw a set of lights dash across the entire horizon within a few seconds, occurring again in the opposite direction just a few moments later.

Reports came flooding in as sightings across the area skyrocketed. Professor Ducker himself claims to have seen these lights as many as twelve times between August and November of that year. Many of his colleagues at the college had similar experiences, as well as hundreds of others in the area.

A Texas Technological College student, Carl Hart, was able to photograph the lights during one evening with a 35-mm Kodak camera. He was paid ten dollars for the photographs that were eventually distributed throughout major media outlets in the nation. Some say they saw the lights in a V-formation while others claimed it was more of a U-formation; but, either way, the reports came to a consensus that these lights were not lights ordinarily seen in the night sky.

Captain Edward J. Rupplet was given the task to investigate and explain these night sky anomalies, but was ultimately unable to give a sufficient answer. He claimed that the lights could have been Plover birds or shooting stars, but those who had seen the lights denied that that was what they saw. Even to this day, the lights over Lubbock that night remain a mystery.

## WAS IT THE JAPANESE OR EXTRATERRESTRIALS?

A little over a month after the attack on Pearl Harbor and America entering the Second World War, fears were high across the cities of the nation. In Los Angeles, on February 24, 1942, searchlights scanned the sky for an object reported to have been floating over the city. Anti-aircraft guns were aimed, air raid sirens wailed through the city streets, and wardens put the city on blackout as the residents of Los Angeles looked into the skies with fear. Everyone thought that a Japanese attack was in the works, but their fears were never fully confirmed.

What was in the sky that night is disputed to this day. Some claim they saw one giant craft slowly lurching over the city, while others claim to have seen a fleet of smaller crafts flying over. Whatever it was, it was soon fired upon by anti-aircraft guns in a barrage of explosions that should have destroyed any modern craft of the day. The craft was shot at for nearly four hours as it moved across the city, causing several buildings to be destroyed and the death of six people in the defense effort.

News reports took off with the story the next morning, claiming it had been a Japanese attack that ended with the fighter planes being destroyed. No evidence was ever found to confirm the account and Japan continues to claim that there was no attack. The next day, the *LA Times* ran a picture of the object lit with searchlights, only causing more confusion. The U.S. Government stated that the panic was caused by "war nerves," although many believe what they saw was extraterrestrial.

## AN EXTRATERRESTRIAL TOUR OF AMERICA

Investigators are looking into two eerily similar UFO reports made within twenty-four hours of each other, although the sightings occurred thousands of miles apart. A California husband and wife living east of Los Angeles were left speechless one night as they looked into the sky to see a gigantic triangular craft silently and slowly flying over them towards the city. Thousands of miles away in Geneva, Ohio, a man saw a similar craft less than twenty-four hours later.

The sighting in California left the couple stunned, feeling like they had just truly experienced a once in a lifetime experience. The anonymous witnesses claim that the craft was completely silent with seven dim lights on its underside.

They claimed that the craft seemed to be sneaking by, trying not to be noticed as it glided in a straight line at about fifty miles per hour. They had no doubt about what they saw. It didn't look like any aircraft or drone they had ever seen, and it definitely didn't move like one either.

The next day in Geneva, Ohio, a local man saw a craft that was eerily similar to the reports coming from Los Angeles, except this time it was headed east and, obviously, much further east than it was the day before. The anonymous witness claimed to have noticed the craft's lights as they were directly overhead of him. He also reported the craft to be triangular in shape with seven lights on the bottom side of the craft—three triangular ones in the middle of the craft with two pairs on each side of the set of three in the center.

He watched the craft move overhead and past the trees until he could no longer see it. Unlike the California reports, the Ohio account reports that the man heard some type of noise coming from the craft that didn't sound like an internal combustion engine or a jet engine, but a constant and steady rumble.

Although both reports were called into the Mutual UFO Network (MUFON), the witnesses were unable to capture a photo of the craft. MUFON will be investigating the claims to see if they are indeed connected in any way.

## TERRESTRIAL MYSTERIES

*Although you may think that humanity's greatest mysteries remain in the skies above you, there are many things of this earth that are just as strange and mysterious. Reports of gigantic creatures seen on open water startle onlookers as the creatures dive back into the depths of Earth's most unexplored areas. Sightings of humungous bipedal creatures scare people enough to keep them out of forests for the rest of their lives. Strange artifacts are found that turn what we know of history upside down. Despite the doubt, there very well may be monsters that inhabit our world, able to stay under the radar of the most curious and adventurous of people.*

*Like ghosts, do these folkloric stories stem from our own existential crises? In the philosophical ponderings of whether we are truly the only intelligent hominids in this world, we may create the mythical creatures that resemble us and hide away in the woods. In the fear-ridden world where predators prey upon the weak, cultures may create monsters in the likeness of those predators. Are the creatures that inhabit folklore, myths, and narratives throughout the world created by overactive imaginations to scare and teach the youth of tomorrow?*

*Most of the time, myths only remain rumors with no evidence to back them up, but sometimes artifacts are found that can only be explained through the paranormal lens. Carcasses of strange beings have been found, molds of gigantic footprints have been made, communal experiences with the paranormal have been corroborated; but still, there are doubts that unhinged imaginations are leading us into the realms of paranormal pseudo-science. If everything in the paranormal realm has been made up, then the biggest mystery remains: why do people fabricate such lies?*

## MAN FINDS BIGFOOT'S TOENAIL

Anyone who's been to northern Arizona knows how beautiful the scenery can be—from the Grand Canyon to the Painted Desert—but they also know how strange the locals can be. Out there in the high desert along the Historic Route 66, it can be a little boring in a town of under five-hundred people, but the locals find ways to pass the time.

A member of the Arizona Cryptozoological Research Organization, Steve Hearn, was recently in Seligman, Arizona, investigating what a recent homebuyer had found on their property: a questionable toenail of the elusive Bigfoot. Although Bigfoot has been discounted as the workings of imaginative minds, people have recorded video and taken pictures of this beast for decades, and now, with this toenail, they believed they had physical proof of Bigfoot's existence. Although it is physical proof of something—maybe insanity—Hearn says they still have quite a bit of work to do in order to attain definitive proof of Bigfoot's presence in the area.

What is most strange is that Hearn claims the DNA analysis of the toenail shows that a human woman mated with a male of an unknown species around thirteen thousand years ago. It might be a little crude, but this is Hearn's idea of Bigfoot's origin story. Hearn himself has spent many decades researching the elusive beast and has seen it himself on the side of the road entering the thickets of the forest.

Although Hearn understands that many people might think he is a little strange, he understands and respects that not all people believe in his research. He will continue to search the high deserts for more evidence, but until the day he finds an actual specimen that leads to irrefutable proof, he will continue to be perceived as the man looking for something that isn't there.

## THE FREAKIEST ADDITION TO
## A FREAKY COLLECTION

California resident and Venice Beach Freakshow owner Todd Ray has quite a freaky collection of taxidermied two-headed animals—such a large collection that he holds the title in the *Guinness Book of World Records*. His collection isn't only about two-headed animals, though. He'll add anything sort of freaky into the mix. He usually gives each addition to his collection a new name, but recently, he received something so freaky he's at a loss for a name.

A man from Arizona called Ray about a body of something he couldn't identify that was found in his backyard, and wondered if Ray would be interested in acquiring it for his collection of freaky beings. Ray was always intrigued by offers like this. Experienced in dealing with people with these claims, Ray told the guy to send him a photo of the thing and he would decide if it made the cut for his show.

Ray never heard back from the guy, but he did receive an unexpected package a few weeks later that contained an absolutely strange body of a creature preserved in rubbing alcohol. Stunned, Ray tried to contact the man he had talked to but there was no return address on the package.

Ray told reporters that this strange being was about a foot long and had gill-like ears below its head, large and diaphanous eyes, a fleshy fang coming out of its mouth, and an appendage like piece of flesh that emerged from above the forehead and wrapped over the head toward its neck. He didn't want to say it was an alien but he really didn't know what to call it at that point.

He contacted many authorities on wildlife and biology to help solve the mystery, but even they had trouble identifying what the creature might have been. A representative from the San Diego Zoo said that the flesh of the creature seemed to be an amalgam of different types of flesh, and that the face was embedded in the section of flesh that is directly behind it—whatever that means. It seemed that even the professionals were trying to grasp how to describe the thing.

No one has reached a conclusion as to what the thing might be. Some say it's a squirrel, others say it's a deformed pig, and even others say that it's a fetal bear still within the amniotic sac. No one knows what it is, but they all have pretty grim conclusions in trying to explain it. Pretty much, at this point, Ray is going to have to get a DNA test done on the creature in order to identify it, name it, and present it to the people as a part of his freak show.

## BIGFOOT ON THE RUN IN THE ROCKIES

Reports of Bigfoot sightings have been spreading throughout Colorado for some time now. From Silverton to Vail, and Fort Collins to Pueblo, Bigfoot seems to get its way around the state, creating unexpected sightings for outdoor enthusiasts in the area. It's mostly legend and folklore, but there are a growing number of believers who only needed one strange experience to change their outlook on life. Kate Murphy couldn't help but to believe in these mountainous rumors after she had an encounter in the woods that took her and her neighbor off guard.

Murphy took a short stroll through the woods with her neighbor. This quiet evening was like any other evening in the Bailey, Colorado area. But as they walked, Murphy and her neighbor heard the sound of branches snapping followed by a seven-foot tall, bipedal creature running away from them through the thicket. In just a few seconds, their disbeliefs in Bigfoot rumors were destroyed by what they stumbled upon in the forest.

Bigfoot sightings number in the hundreds in the Bailey, Colorado area alone, with a high concentration in the Rocky Mountain Range that crosses the state from north to south.

Cryptozoologists find Murphy's report credible because both her and her neighbor confirm what they saw, but there is no video proof to provide hard evidence of what they encountered. How should we think of people who claim to have seen Bigfoot? Should we consider them a little off kilter, or should we take what they're saying with a grain of salt and try to swallow their paranormal concoction?

Either way, there is a reason why so many people are becoming believers in the paranormal, and that's because more and more people are encountering the strange and don't know how to understand it. These experiences are life changing and make you question everything that you've believed, giving you phenomenological—although subjective—evidence of something rarely seen.

### GIGANTIC SEA CREATURE EMERGED FROM THE DEPTHS, STARTLED ONLOOKERS

Although we often ponder what types of life there are out there in the universe, there are creatures of this earth that are still as foreign and mysterious as the life-forms we suspect inhabit the skies above us. The oceans and deep waters of Earth are truly the last frontier of exploration for humanity, containing mysteries in their benthic waters that can baffle people when they emerge into the light of day. A recent find on the shores of Lake Macquarie in New South Wales, Australia, has presented new evidence of the mysteries the waters of the world hold.

New South Wales resident Ethan Tipper found the carcass of an unknown sea creature washed up on the shore of Lake Macquarie. The creature had a twenty-foot-long body of an eel, a dolphin-like head, and an elongated jaw with sharp teeth. Tipper went online with the photo to gather consensus of what the creature might be. He received many responses including accusations that the photo was Photoshopped to create a commotion, but he confirmed that the photo was untouched and accurate with what he had found that day. Aside from the skeptics and naysayers, Tipper didn't gain any insight from the online community.

A museum fish collector, Mark McGrouther, had the best explanation for the creature. Although he has never seen one in the flesh before, McGrouther suspects that the large creature may be a pike eel—which inhabit deep waters off of the east coast of Australia. He suspects that a crew of fisherman caught a little more than they bargained for and ended up discarding the creature upon their return to shore.

Although it seems probable that this strange sea creature is what he claims it is, pike eels are only reported to grow about five feet long—which is much smaller than the creature that was found by Tipper that day. Maybe the eel was an apex predator with no competition around, letting it grow to a size much larger than the average size of a pike eel. Maybe it wasn't a pike eel at all and some type of deep-sea creature not yet known by biologists. Or maybe Tipper is throwing us all for a loop with his fantastic Photoshop skills. We'll never know, but this report is sure to cause us to second guess what we know and what we don't know about the inhabitants of the waters around us.

## YES, 911? I SAW BIGFOOT!

A Bedford County, Virginia, woman called 911 for an emergency. It wasn't because she had witnessed a robbery, or that she had been threatened or attacked, but because she reportedly saw Bigfoot on the side of the road holding an infant Bigfoot. Taken off guard as she was driving, she was obviously unable to snap a photo of the sighting, but she thought it would be best to call the authorities immediately. After all, who wants a seven-foot, hairy creature carrying their children throughout town and causing a ruckus?

Like many people calling in with fantastic stories, the woman began the 911 call with "I know this may sound crazy but . . . I saw Bigfoot." She was right though, it does sound a little crazy to say you saw Bigfoot carrying a baby Bigfoot down the road. Although she had been scared beyond belief, she went back the next day to find footprints that were at least twice the size of her own feet with a stride that she couldn't even walk along with.

The police in the area didn't really know how to respond. They don't get reports like this very often, but they always appreciate those heroes who take the time to report suspicious activity in their area. This Virginia woman is an unsung hero that wished to remain anonymous in order to keep her name untarnished from Bigfoot rumors. Similar situations in the area have either never occurred or continue to go unreported by the public, while this case has provided no physical or photo evidence to confirm the sighting.

## WEREWOLVES MOSTLY KEPT OUT OF GERMANY, MOSTLY

Werewolf sightings may be the least reported sightings out of all the paranormal experiences one can stumble upon. Maybe it's not too often that you find yourself alone at night in the German or English countryside during a full moon; or maybe you do and you've just gotten lucky so far. German towns have been plagued with folklore of werewolves for a long time, and in 1988, one report of the infamous Morbach Monster had locals in a panic when their safeguard failed them.

The folklore around the Morbach Monster dates back to the early 19th century as a fighter in Napoleon's army deserted the war effort with a group of Russians near the village of Wittlich, Germany. During his sojourn in the German countryside away from battle, Thomas Johannes Baptist Schwytzer attacked and killed a local farmer and his wife. But, rumors say the wife was able to curse the man before she was killed.

What was the curse, you ask? Well, purportedly the woman cursed the man to wander full-mooned nights as a beast, terrifying and killing anyone who was unlucky enough to cross paths with it. The story goes that the villagers set out one full moon, fed up with the terror, to hunt, capture, and destroy the beast before it destroyed them. The hunt was a success. They put an end to the beast's reign of terror. But they could not guarantee that it wouldn't come back, so they created a shrine in which to burn candles during a full moon, thwarting the beast from entering the town.

Nearly two hundred years later, the candle still burned through the evenings every twenty-nine days. A full-mooned night in 1988 saw this safeguard fail, scaring the ranks of U.S. military men occupying a base nearby. The soldiers had all heard the local rumors of werewolves and knew about the shrine that kept them away, but as they passed the shrine that night they noticed the candle had gone out. Not taking any of the local lore seriously, they joked about how the werewolf would inevitably be seen that night.

Later that night, the Morbach U.S. Air Force Base was awoken to sirens signaling that the perimeter of the base had been breached. One soldier who kept guard said he saw a large beast trying to get past the gates, but it then ran back into the forest as the spotlight was shone upon it.

In an uproar, the men went searching for the monster. Search dogs had their nose to the ground and obviously had a scent to follow, but at a certain point, the dogs would lead no further. The dogs seemed reluctant to continue the hunt, which obviously also took the fire out of the soldiers' motivation as well. The men turned back to the base that night with their eyes watching behind them, filled with a new respect for German folklore. What was it that they tried to find that night? Was it really the Morbach Monster coming back after nearly two hundred years to feast on the villagers and U.S. military men? Or was it just a tale believed a little too much by the locals?

# CHAPTER 8:
# FLOCK MENTALITY FAILS

No one wants to be called a sheep, but somehow being a black sheep is no better. Either way you look at it, being a part of a group and being apart from a group both hold negative connotations that not everyone wants to identify with. You don't want to be seen as one of many, falling in line, following and believing what you are told, but you also don't want to be an outsider who has no one to relate to. How should one deal with peer pressure without seeming too willing to please one's peers? Where one stands amongst their cohorts is a precarious position, obscuring whether we should consider ourselves an individual or a part of a greater whole.

As you ponder your relationships with others, it can get awfully messy awfully quick. Sometimes you might not ponder enough, and you find yourself following a group of people into an embarrassing situation that you could have avoided in the first place if you would have thought for yourself. You realize you shouldn't have gone with your friends to the latest Britney Spears concert as reporters interview you after the show about how much you liked it. You realize that you shouldn't have told your friends that you think the president isn't an American citizen before you did your own research. You can be led astray quite easily when popular opinion seems to be the consensus of truth, but you shouldn't believe everything you are told.

Locals inherently think of themselves as a part of a group that includes all of the other locals that live in their area. People throughout the world identify with each other in their dreams, desires, and interests, but sometimes those groups can be led astray. Every person is a part of a group, but it's how much you let the group define you that can create situations you don't want to be a part of. Remember, no matter how much you inundate yourself with the people around you and their opinions, it's never too late to jump ship and start swimming by yourself. If you miss the opportunity to bail, you just might find yourself in an embarrassing situation where people view you as another sheep in the flock. The only flocks one should dedicate themselves to are the flocks that tend to the individual and the cold hard truth.

## FLOCKS LEARNING VALUABLE LESSONS THROUGHOUT HISTORY

*There is a popular saying that states something about those who do not know the past are destined to repeat it. Well, you can pretty much take that saying as a general truth. It makes you think about how many people sat around doing the same stupid stuff over and over again before there was recorded history. Maybe that's why narratives and storytelling became an art: in order to make sure we are somewhat aware of all the stupid groups of people and their ill-informed decisions that came before us.*

*Through history, you can learn that millions of people can all be equally influenced to do horrible things to other groups of people. You can learn about all of the false testaments of truth accepted without evidence or test results. You can learn about all of the stupid acts people have committed as they blindly followed their fellows. Take some lessons from colonial America or revolutionary France to learn how much people can be influenced by anger or fear or just plain apathy to justice. Many people have been sacrificed at the altar of ideology, so let's make sure to not be led there again.*

## REVOLUTIONARY LEADER LOSES HIS HEAD

Marie Antoinette may be one of the most famous victims of mob mentality, but during the French Revolution, she was only one of about fifty thousand people who were executed for supposed treason and counter-revolutionary plotting.

Once the downtrodden citizens of France were worked into a frenzy about social injustice, the executions committed by the revolutionists became a regular event, with not even women or children spared from witnessing the violence. It was a struggle between the exploited proletariat and the complacent bourgeoisie that erupted into the beheading of oppressors and all of those who spoke out against the revolution.

And the guillotine wasn't the only method used: victims were beaten, faced firing squads, and were thrown from boats with weights tied to them, just to name a few of the other terrors unleashed on counter-revolutionists. Although aristocrats were frequently targeted, they weren't the only victims.

The revolutionists used any arbitrary reason to round up those they felt weren't loyal to their cause. And few of the victims were given fair trials—if they were given trials at all. After almost a year of fear and executions, the people started to realize that their revolutionary leader had turned into a murderous fanatic, and in true mob fashion, they solved the problem with one last beheading.

## THE WITCH HUNT BEGINS

Perhaps one of the most famous examples of flock mentality gone wrong is the 1692 Salem Witch Trials. It's an example of just how dangerous mass hysteria can be. Even now, more than three centuries later, the phrase "witch hunt" is still used when we talk about someone who is being accused without reason.

It all began when a girl named Betty Parris started behaving strangely, running around, diving under furniture, contorting in pain, and complaining of fever. Soon, several of her friends began exhibiting the same symptoms. A doctor was unable to find any cause for the girls' behaviors, which is now theorized to have been anything from stress and boredom to delusional psychosis. But the doctor in Salem suggested a much different cause—witchcraft.

The number of girls acting strangely continued to grow, and some of them even claimed to have seen "witches flying through the winter mist." The girls began pointing fingers at women in the community, and the fear in the town grew out of control. Officials began arresting anyone who was suspected of being a witch, no matter how ridiculous the "evidence" was. They even went so far as to arrest four-year-old Dorcas Good and imprison her for eight months.

One of the most bizarre parts of the Salem Witch Trials was the absurd methods used to determine whether someone was a witch. Judges actually permitted things like "spectral evidence," which was testimony from someone who claimed to be visited by a witch's specter, and the inane "touching test," where defendants were asked to touch an afflicted person to see if their contortions and fits would stop.

By the time the hysteria died down in Salem, around one hundred fifty people had been imprisoned and twenty-five of the accused were killed.

## EARLY SETTLERS USE FIRST NATION TRIBES AS SCAPEGOAT

In an early instance of flock mentality, Mormons in Utah in 1857 ran across a wagon train of families on their way to California. No one is exactly sure why, but for some reason the church members felt threatened by the travelers, banded together, and decided to attack them.

But they didn't want to be blamed for the attack, so they disguised themselves as Native Americans, and recruited some Paiute Indians to help them out. The ambushed travelers defended themselves for five days, after which the so-called "Mormon Militia" approached with white flags to signal a truce. The travelers accepted, hoping for basic provisions as they were taken into Mormon protection. But as soon as they surrendered, the mob once again turned on them and murdered the last of them.

The incident has been a source of shame within the Mormon community, who initially denied their role in the massacre, blaming the Paiute Indians. But eventually, Mormon leaders admitted that the Mormon Militia participated, although they emphasized that Brigham Young, the church's prophet and president at the time, was not involved. Today, the church maintains a monument in the meadow where the massacre occurred to honor those who were murdered.

## STUDY CLAIMS: A THIRD OF PEOPLE AGREE WITH EVERYONE AROUND THEM

In 1953, psychologist Solomon Asch set up an experiment to see how often people conform to those around them. Subjects were told they were being given a vision test, and then asked simple questions with obvious answers. But what the subjects weren't told was that the other people in the room were in on the experiment, and were told to give wrong answers.

With only one subject actually being tested in the experiment, the other "subjects" were used to try to influence the real subject's answers by answering the questions incorrectly. One question asked the subject to match a given line with the line that is the same length as it. The answer was extremely obvious, but the sway of the fake subjects' wrong answers led the actual subjects to answer incorrectly as well.

Asch discovered that thirty-two percent of people gave incorrect answers when everyone else around them also gave the incorrect answers. Even when the correct answer was plainly obvious, nearly a third of the subjects went along with the group.

Asch's experiment showed how social pressure can change opinion—and even change our perceptions of facts! Do people tend to believe obviously erroneous information because many of their peers believe it and tell them it is true? Or can we use our social influence to sway people toward the truth?

## NO TIME TO PRACTICE WHAT THEY PREACH

The biblical story of the Good Samaritan is an allegory of how people should treat and react to people who are in need. The story tells of a man on the side of the road near the brink of death who is passed by multiple travelers who refuse to help him, except for one man who takes the needy man in to help him heal. People have used this story to tell a moral in how we should treat strangers, and recently, two psychologists decided to use this story's framework to see how it affects the actions of religious people.

Pscychologists John Darley and C. Daniel Batson gathered a group of seminary students as their subjects. The researchers would conduct an experiment to see if the story had any influence on the seminary students' actions. Half of the seminary subjects were given the subject of the Good Samaritan to deliver a sermon on at Mass, while the other half were directed to give a sermon on the job opportunities at the seminary.

The twist is that while the seminary students were on their way to Mass, they would pass by a man in need in the alley behind the church. The sermons were to be held at different times, giving some students more time to prepare and others less time to prepare, causing some to be more in a hurry than others.

Results of the study show that people who recently studied the biblical allegory were not more likely to help the man in the alley. Both groups of people reacted in a similar fashion, but the one factor that correlated with whether the student would help or not was how much time they had.

If the students were pressed for time to make it to their sermon, only ten percent of them would stop to help the man, even if they were on their way to give a sermon on the same exact situation. Time determined whether the subjects would act morally in accordance with the story or not. The study shows that we have a high proclivity to not practice what we preach in those situations. Turns out that it might be a little more comfortable to speak about helping the needy as opposed to actually acting and helping those in need.

## THE INTERNET BRINGING THE FLOCKS TOGETHER

*The invention of the internet was a history changing event, but its clear cut into the future was a double-edged sword. Once thought to be the key to public knowledge, the internet can now be seen as a propagator of lies and fallacies as well. People acquire their information of current events from succinct memes that tell us little of the facts. People read headlines as content and claim to know the details. Reports on all types of studies claim a million different things to be the truth from the same set of data. How can anyone claim to know the truth with so much obfuscation of the truth?*

*The internet brings knowledge to the people and it can also bring hordes of people together with common goals. You can use the internet to sign petitions to the government, or you can use the internet to gather people together to pull a massive prank on unsuspecting victims. There are the good things the internet gives its users and there are bad things. With the ability to stay anonymous on the internet, people are posting whatever they want to the internet to influence people into doing or believing things they never would have in the first place.*

*Flash mobs meet on the streets of a city to create civil unrest or confusion. Online profile users unite under a thread regardless of whether it is valid or not. People can be led to do some crazy things, but it's when the internet is used as a tool to gather and influence people to do crazy things that we need to start questioning the internet's history changing authority.*

## HUNGRY FOR COMPETITION

In 2013, a flash mob that organized itself through social media and met at the Mall of Louisiana in Baton Rouge took an ugly turn, causing an evacuation of the shopping center.

Around two hundred young people gathered in the food court at around 6:00 p.m. Soon after, three separate police agencies were called to the scene with reports of a fight.

An unnamed witness told reporters that she was in the food court with her child when she saw some of the teenagers start fighting. When they started overturning tables and jumping over them, the woman grabbed her child and ran.

"I grabbed my son and took off running, but all the doors to the stores were closed," she said. "I ran through a side door into the parking lot and ran around trying to find my car."

Police shut down the mall for the rest of the night so they could contain the situation. Although no one was hurt, shoppers were unsettled by the riot. One Twitter user asked, "Since when did the Mall of Louisiana food court turn into *The Hunger Games?*"

## FICTIONAL TALE PROMPTS
## NON-FICTIONAL RESPONSE

Elan Gale is a TV producer from Los Angeles, California, who apparently decided to produce his own little story when he was on a US Airways flight during Thanksgiving in 2013.

Gale tweeted several times about a woman named Diane, who was supposedly sitting in seat 7A and was being rude to flight attendants. Eventually, he retaliated by writing her a nasty note on a napkin. He took a photo of it, and also posted it to Twitter.

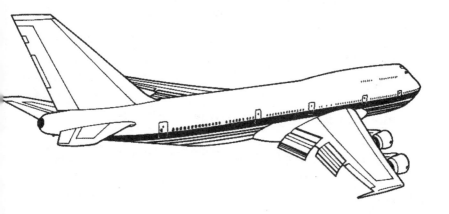

The "fight" continued, with Gale tweeting things like, "I'm not going to lie, I am shaking. This is so terrifying. She is so angry at me it's kind of incredible," and describing his fellow passenger as "in her late forties or early fifties. She is wearing mom jeans and a studded belt and she is wearing a medical mask over her idiot face."

Diane eventually wrote her own note, and Gale tweeted more barbs and insults. All the while, Gale's Twitter followers grew from thirty thousand to around one hundred thousand, with people cheering him on and praising him for his tactics.

The alleged fight culminated after the flight ended, with Gale tweeting, "Well, Diane just slapped me."

Four days later, Gale took to Twitter again to reveal that the entire thing had been a hoax. There was no passenger named Diane. He simply made everything up for its entertainment value. But the disturbing thing about Gale's Thanksgiving tweets is just how many people jumped on his bandwagon and cheered him on. Gale was publicly berating a stranger—whether imaginary or not—who his followers knew nothing about. His Twitter audience heard only his side of the story, yet they applauded his rude insults and jumped to the conclusion that Diane deserved this treatment.

### FANS OF NU METAL ARE TRICKED AGAIN

In April of 2016, an event on Facebook had Ohio residents and fans of the fleeting 90s nu metal music scene getting excited about the reunion of a seminal band of the genre. The event claimed that Limp Bizkit would be hitting the stage again at a gas station in Dayton.

The group of 90s superstars were slotted to play at the Sunoco Station in a small Midwest town on a Wednesday evening, and people were pumped. Promo posters spread around town and on Dayton Facebook circles, and nearly eight thousand people confirmed that they would be attending the show. They couldn't wait to sing along to the band's original classics like "Faith" and "Nookie."

Tweets from Fred Durst himself—lead singer of the band—refuted the reports that Limp Bizkit would be playing in Dayton. Even posts from Dayton's city government were sent out and a sign was posted on the front door of the gas station to assure everyone that the rumors were false. People just didn't listen though.

Although authorities and the band themselves let everyone know that the show was a hoax and to not show up, hundreds of Limp Bizkit fans showed up at the gas station that Wednesday evening. They still had faith that they'd be able to see Fred and his red Yankees hat moshing on the stage with Wes Borland acting and looking like some type of monster behind his guitar. None of their beliefs came to fruition. But the cops did show up after hundreds of fans gathered in front of the gas station.

## SURFING THE CESSPOOL OF THE INTERNET

If you saw this story on social media, there's a good chance you'd share it with your friends without even reading it, according to a study published in June 2016. Researchers discovered that of more than fifty-nine thousand articles shared on Twitter from sites like the *BBC*, *Huffington Post*, *New York Times*, *Fox News*, and

*CNN*, fifty-nine percent of them were never clicked. So the people sharing the articles didn't actually read them first.

In a press release, the study's authors say that sharing an article and actually reading it are "poorly correlated."

"People are more willing to share an article than read it," study co-author Arnaud Legout says. "This is typical of modern information consumption. People form an opinion based on a summary, or a summary of summaries, without making the effort to go deeper."

The study also discovered that while Twitter users do see the links when they're posted by news sites, the users are far more likely to click on a link if its posted by another Twitter user. Twitter also helps prolong the lifespan of news stories, with eighteen percent of clicks on links coming after the story has been posted more than a week.

The *Washington Post* sums up the findings pretty well by saying that they shed light upon "so much of the oft-demoralizing cesspool that is internet culture."

## ELEVEN-YEAR-OLD THIEVES NOT FOUND TO BE FUNNY OR CUTE

In 2011, dozens of young men in Philadelphia, Pennsylvania, ran into a Sears department store as part of a flash-mob and stole thousands of dollars' worth of merchandise.

Police believed that the group organized their activity through social media, traveling together on public transportation and arriving at the store at the same time.

Police Superintendent Michael Chitwood said that about forty boys between the ages of eleven and nineteen arrived at the store and began to "rob, steal, and pillage."

Officers were able to catch sixteen of the suspects. Most of them were juveniles who were released to the custody of their parents, but a nineteen-year-old was charged with retail theft and corrupting the morals of a minor.

Chitwood said, "When this mob mentality comes to a community and robs a village, there has to be consequences. That's the only way you're going to stop this."

He added, "People have to realize this is not condoned, funny, or cute. It's criminal. Period. If you've got an eleven-year-old involved in this type of mob mentality, what are they going to be doing when they are sixteen?"

## THE HORRIBLE AND EMBARRASSING THINGS FLOCKS DO AND DON'T DO

*Whether it's doing something horrendous or not doing something about something horrendous, flock mentality can make people act erratically or not at all. Sometimes you might not know you are a part of a group, but may find out that a majority of people acted the same way you did, influenced by the same false statements as you were. Whether you act alike or not, you can still be considered part of a flock that has followed an idea or supposed truth mindlessly.*

*One easy way to determine whether you are following the pack or anything other than yourself is to ask yourself one thing: Am I doing this because I want to, or am I doing this because I'm afraid of what people will think if I don't. Or you can ask yourself whether you don't do something becasue you're afraid of what others may think. Either way, it is yourself you must follow if you don't want to turn out like these locals who followed the pack a little too far.*

## MAN MAKES MILLIONS BY LEAVING NO STONE UNSOLD

In 1975, people willingly plunked down nearly $4—a lot of money for that day and age—for a strange fad that was popular during the Christmas season: the Pet Rock.

Creator Gary Dahl had heard some friends complaining about having to take care of their pets, and he had an idea for a "perfect pet." A pet that would need zero care whatsoever, and would "live" forever. What was this perfect pet? The perfect pet was a rock that needed no food, water, light, or care, just a nice spot for it to sit for the rest of its almost eternal life.

Dahl imported rocks from Mexico's Rosarito Beach, and then packaged them in boxes with air holes and a bed of straw. He even included an instruction booklet on how to care for the Pet Rock.

While it seems like consumers may have wasted their money on such a silly trend, Dahl himself is probably one person who was happy with the flock mentality of Pet Rock purchasers. Although it was only popular for a few months, Dahl ultimately sold around five million rocks and lived out the rest of his life as a millionaire.

## ELMO DABBLES IN COMMODITY TRADING

In 1996, children all over the country who loved Sesame Street knew exactly what they wanted for Christmas. Tyco Toys introduced Tickle Me Elmo, a fuzzy red doll that giggled hysterically when its stomach was touched, and suddenly, the country went crazy for Elmo.

Merchants could barely keep the doll on their shelves, with everyone wanting a Tickle Me Elmo for their children for the holidays. And then, people started realizing that they could take advantage of other people's desperation for the toy. Auctions and raffles were held, and some people even offered to sell the $30 toy for ridiculously marked up prices, sometimes as much as $2,000.

At a Walmart in Texas, two employees were fired after they hid a few of the dolls from customers so they could buy them themselves. Mob boss John Gotti's son reportedly paid $8,000 at a toy store in New York City for an entire case of the toys. And the frenzy even crossed the border into Canada, where a crowd of nearly three hundred Elmo-seekers in Frederickton, New Brunswick, stampeded into a store and trampled an employee, who had to be hospitalized.

It was obvious to many that Elmo mania went too far. One family in Maryland even donated $800 to charity so they could use a steamroller to squash one of the frenzy-inducing toys. A radio station sponsored the event, and assured listeners that they were still supporters of Elmo and Sesame Street. But, they said, "it amazes us that his positive message has been lost on greedy parents who have been taken in by the hype-driven media."

## DON'T RELY ON THE COMMON GOOD

In 2004, traffic cameras captured a sad scene when at least a dozen drivers swerved around a woman laying unconscious and bleeding on a road in London.

The footage shows car after car passing by the twenty-five-year-old woman, who was lying face down with her head near the curb.

A bus driver finally stopped to help, and the woman was taken to a London hospital. Unfortunately, she was unable to remember what caused her injury.

A statement from Scotland Yard said, "Officers recovered good quality CCTV footage from a 321 bus, which clearly shows drivers swerving to avoid the woman—who was bleeding profusely from a head wound and lying unconscious next to the curb."

A commenter on the BBC News website summed up the actions of the apathetic drivers with this comment: "Our attitudes and civility to our common man has gone, gone for good. How sad." Are we no longer able to rely on our fellow citizens in our most desperate of times? Although we might be a little squeamish of blood, especially in public places, we should still have the decency to be able to talk to the people around us and ask if they need help. There may be millions of people in need in London, but this woman was most definitely in need of help when no one was willing to provide it.

## NORTH DAKOTA'S POPULATION DOUBLES IN ONE WEEKEND

In 1969, Chuck Stroup was a North Dakota State University student who was upset that he couldn't make the trip to Fort Lauderdale, Florida for spring break. So he decided to throw his own spring break festivities in the tiny town of Zap, North Dakota, population of 250.

Stroup put ads in student newspapers across the country that encouraged people to "Zip to Zap" for spring break, and the town itself publicized the event, thinking it would be great for the town's economy. But word of the event spread much more quickly than anyone anticipated, and soon 3,000 college kids showed up to the small town.

NDSU's newspaper prophetically advertised the Zip to Zap event as a "full program of orgies, brawls, freak-outs, and arrests." The town was unable to handle the spring breakers' requests for beer, so restaurant owners began doubling their prices in an effort to slow down the drinkers' consumption. This only angered the drunk mob, who began rioting and destroying the town. The North Dakota National Guard had to be called in to calm things down, but by the time they arrived, most of the students were passed out and hung over.

## PANIC IN ORLANDO

On Christmas Day 2015, families at Disney World in Orlando, Florida, were panicked when a fistfight was somehow mistaken for shots fired.

Orange County Sheriff Office spokeswoman Deputy Lourdes Clayton told reporters that the fight started on the second floor of the Bongos Cuban Café restaurant, and the commotion may have sounded like a gunshot.

Panic broke out, as parents grabbed their children and hid inside shops and restaurants. Police swept the area known as "Downtown Disney" for a shooter, but quickly realized it was a false alarm.

Still, the incident shook up many visitors. Melissa Paz was one of the parents enjoying the day at the theme park when the mass hysteria erupted.

"There was a stampede at the Lego store at Disney Springs," she said. "Luckily we were only on the outside area of the store and were able to shield the kids from the mob. Shaken, but not a scratch on us."

Clayton reported that one person was arrested in relation to the fight and charged with disorderly conduct.

Reedy Creek Fire and Rescue Deputy Chief Eric Ferrari said the shooting report was a "total false alarm." He added, "Everyone is on edge in general. I guess it started a mass panic."

## PARKING ON THIN ICE

A tradition at Lake Geneva's Winterfest is for the festival-goers to park on the frozen ice of the lake in order to alleviate congested streets and to skip over parking fares for the day. But when winter isn't as cold as it traditionally is, a tradition like parking on a frozen lake can become dangerous, costly, and embarrassing.

The 2016 Winterfest was punctuated with an event that has never happened before. Dozens of cars parked on the ice broke through the thin layer and began sinking into the water. None of the cars fully sunk, but many were engine deep in the water before they could be saved. People attended that day to watch the snow sculpting contest, but ended up seeing a better show than they imagined. A tow truck retrieved the vehicles and no one was injured during the incident.

## POLL TO NAME RESEARCH VESSEL FAILS

The United Kingdom's most recent addition to their fleet of research vessels has been having difficulty in finding a name. Britain's Natural Environment Research Council aren't receiving any legitimate help since they opened polls to the public to help decide the name of the vessel. The council wanted a respectful name that would reflect the mission and the hundreds of millions of dollars that have gone into the research, but they haven't received one yet.

The council turned to the public in hope that they would help decide between the name of one great scientist or explorer and another, but as the polls closed, their hopes were dashed. The winning name was Boaty McBoatface with a whopping 124,109 votes—beating its closest competitor by nearly 40,000 votes.

British Broadcasting Channel radio host James Hand originally proposed the name because he thought it was a brilliant name, but he now apologizes for the controversy. He didn't even vote for the name when came down to it. Boaty Mcboatface was so popular he might as well have thrown away his vote when he voted for naturalist David Attenborough.

## POLL TO CHANGE SCHOOL NAME FAILS

Robert E. Lee Elementary School in Austin, Texas, was in need of a new name. It wanted something relevant and inspirational and chosen by the people to represent their community. The school administration decided to create an open poll for the people to decide what the school would be named.

Although residents thought the former name was a little offensive and that it shouldn't be associated with an educational institution, the names that were chosen to replace the original were really no better. The names in the running included Donald J. Trump, Harper Lee, Spike Lee, Bruce Lee, and even The Adolf Hitler School for Friendship and Tolerance.

Some of the names were more popular than others, with Trump taking the lead with nearly forty-five votes. Harper Lee came in second with thirty votes, with the Adolf Hitler School for Friendship and Tolerance—unfortunately—in third place with eight votes. There were also thirty-four votes in support of keeping the original name. The school administration were a little disheartened by their effort to change their school's name and results showed little hope for a positive result.

# CHAPTER 9:
# STUCK IN EMBARRASSING SITUATIONS

Some situations are more embarrassing than others. You could be walking down an icy sidewalk and take a good fall on a slick spot, but if no one is around, it's like nothing happened. You could finish eating nachos and still have some cheese on your face, and if someone brings it to your attention, it can be as if you died right then and there from embarrassment.

Sometimes you can get yourself into situations that are easy to get into, but once it's time to get out, you can't. Sometimes you have dirty little secrets that go flying into the public eye without you realizing. People begin asking questions about what you were doing and they start snooping for the dirt. Sometimes, you're embarrassed by your family members who don't really know the definition of personal space or boundaries. The lines that separate what you think should be public knowledge and what you think should be kept secret are quite obscure. All it takes is a situation where people start asking questions and the most embarrassing information is revealed to the light of day—well, either that or you're stuck hanging in a tree with no one around to help.

Don't get yourself stuck or hung up about being embarrassed. Take some hints from the following stories on how to stay away from these situations or how to act when you find yourself in the middle of embarrassment. The following locals made it through national headlines making them the butt of a joke, while their reputations were only slightly tarnished. Remember: embarrassment isn't the end of the world, but when it makes headline news, it sure can feel that way.

## LOCALS GETTING INTO STUFF THEY SHOULDN'T, AND THEN GETTING STUCK

*It is common to get stuck in bad situations or between a rock and a hard place if you don't look out for your future, but it's much easier to get stuck in a household appliance or in a tree. Locals throughout the world are always getting caught in awkward situations—some legal, some not.*

*One thing is for sure, people always seem to get stuck in windows and doors that they should not be trying to go through. If something is locked, it's usually good practice to take note that whoever closed it up thought it was obviously not suitable for someone to go through, but people often disregard this signifier. Some might think that they can go anywhere they want without repercussions, and some might not know how to tell if they should go somewhere or not. Whichever way you approach the warning signs to stay out, you have a pretty good chance of getting stuck in something that you thought you would be able to get out of. And once you're stuck, you're a perfect model for all of those social-media photographers just looking for that next funny photo to post on their online account. Don't be that person. Read the signs and know how to keep yourself out of sticky situations before you get stuck.*

## BROKEN DOOR, USE FRONT ENTRANCE

A man trying to break into a Rent-A-Car facility in Brockton, Massachusetts, got stuck for nearly nine hours under the roll-up metal door he was trying to crawl under. The owner of the store came to work in the morning to find Manuel Fernandes' head sticking out from the bottom of the door. Fernandes' looked like he was just about ready to give up on everything. He had been lying there for nine hours, so his seeming lack of ambition or drive makes sense.

The owner called the cops and snapped a few photos— and a video—of the would-be burglar lying there with nowhere to go. He told Fernandes to hold tight until the cops got there. The cops figured it all out and clarified Fernandes' story for him. Fenandes told the cops he got stuck as he was trying to fix the door, but the cops didn't buy it. He was charged with attempted robbery, and his embarrassing situation became very popular amongst the online community.

## ENGLISH MAN LEFT HANGING

A student of Nottingham Trent University in England was caught in an awkward situation when he got stuck upside down in a window he was trying to crawl through. Not only is it embarrassing enough to be hanging upside down from a window—unable to free yourself from the situation—but it only gets worse when you're stuck there for five hours with your butt and genitals exposed.

Two students of the university were strolling about the campus that morning as they noticed a pair of legs jetting out from the side of a window. Upon further inspection, they found a man hanging there with almost his whole body through the window except for his feet, which were stuck in the window frame, leaving the man to dangle for hours and hours until he was discovered.

The only problem is, the two students who found him didn't call for help automatically. They knew a good photo opportunity when they saw one, so they continued by taking a few selfies in front of this embarrassed man left hanging.

Authorities and help crews eventually arrived, but like the two students, they needed to take a few pictures too before they got to work. Eventually, after hours of being caught in the window, hanging upside down, the man was taken down to let the blood rush away from his embarrassed face.

## HOW TO REFRAME
## CONCEPTIONS OF ART WITH TREES

A Norwegian student of the University for the Creative Arts in London, Hilde Krohn Huse, had stumbled on a conceptual goldmine during a project she filmed for class. Unfortunately, during the project, Huse was left hanging in a tree naked in the woods, almost outside the earshot of anyone that could save her.

Don't get us wrong, she didn't plan something else and then somehow ended up being naked and hanging by her feet from a tree. Her original plan was to make a movie of herself hanging naked from a tree, but what she didn't consider was how to get out of her harness and down from the tree. She hung for nearly thirty minutes, yelling into the forest for help. Lucky for her, she didn't go too far off the beaten path because a friend heard her and came running to help.

For most, it's not ideal to hang yourself from a tree naked because it seems like you're some type of bait for the ravenous predators around, but Huse didn't worry about that. Obviously, she didn't worry about too much other than the concept of her film—which ended up changing as things went wrong.

Huse felt an incredible unease and sense of anxiety as she watched the film for the first time, but she also realized that the film wasn't all that bad. With a change in its conceptual framework, the video could still be just as artistically competent. The video was accepted in the Bloomberg New Contemporary exhibition, which provides a platform for thirty-seven recent graduates of art programs in the UK to present their work to the public.

The piece "Hanging in the Woods" is now a conceptual film in which the boundaries between performance and reality break down, and the power of the artist over their piece of art becomes non-existent. Huse has helped us all realize the conceptual power behind contemporary art. Although the process and product of art making might not go as planned, the artist can always change the framework in which they operate to keep things relevant and not embarrassing.

## MAN GETS A GOOD HEAD
## CLEANING IN WASHING MACHINE

A Chinese man from the Fujian Province was recently saved by authorities from a running washing machine. Apparently, the unnamed man was trying to fix his

washing machine in mid-cycle when his head—somehow inside the machine at the time—got stuck. The man's roommates tried to free his head from the contraption, but had failed and then called the authorities. The fire department tried for nearly forty minutes before they had to resort to a circular saw.

The man was covered with fire resistant materials to prevent his clothes from catching fire as sparks showered down on him. They were eventually able to free the man from the machine but the machine itself could not be saved. The man is reported to have only received minor head injuries while the washing machine is no longer in commission.

# FAMILY SITUATIONS THAT COULDN'T GET MORE AWKWARD

*When you were in high-school, your mother used to drop you off at school, calling out to you from her wood-paneled PT Cruiser as you walked up to the building, "I love you, Spudly!!" You would turn around in horror to find that all of your peers were watching your mother wave to you and drive off in that hideous car. It's not that she did this to embarrass you, but because she cared for you and loved you—hopefully. The combinations of your nickname (Spudly), your mother's unabashed enthusiasm for her love for you, and that freaking car really put the icing on the cake of embarrassment for you. That's all behind you now, but you of all people know how much an embarrassing memory can haunt someone.*

*There's no saying what will embarrass a person, but one consistent factor that causes embarrassment is family. Their unbounded love leads them into a fit of excitement that can make a fool out of James Dean. It's not that love is embarrassing, but the emotions that stem and emerge from the feelings of love lead people into an enraptured state that is fit only for the caricatures of comic strips. Take some lessons from these locals whose families ended being the cause of their embarrassment.*

## FOOTBALL COACH'S AFFAIR COMES CRASHING DOWN

Sometimes we have secrets we don't want anyone to know, and sometimes those secrets are destined to be known. Arkansas' Razorbacks' coach Bobby Petrino had one such secret that was soon to become common knowledge after a motorcycle accident he was involved in. Petrino sustained broken ribs and neck injuries, but the most severe damage would later affect his marriage.

Although Petrino said he had been riding his motorcycle alone along the two-lane highway, patrolmen revealed that he indeed had a passenger with him, twenty-five-year-old Jessica Dorrell, who was an employee for the university's football program. Dorrell was not only Petrino's passenger, but also his mistress. Petrino's secret affair with the employee was about to be revealed to the public, and he knew he had to make a few phones calls before the news broke.

Petrino called Arkansas athletic director Jeff Long and told him that he had been in a wreck, claiming that as he came out of the ditch he crashed into, a woman, Dorrell, was on the side of the road flagging people down for help. What he didn't reveal to Long was that Dorrell had been his passenger. Petrino was later put on leave as details of the two's love affair came to light.

Petrino was obviously concerned about protecting his family from the stories of his infidelity, but he was obviously not so concerned about the effect his infidelity would have on his family. Petrino said he was now working on repairing his relationship with his family and the university, while his motorcycle was laid to waste in the nearest junkyard.

## GRANDFATHER AND GRANDSON CAN'T REMEMBER WHAT THE OTHER LOOKS LIKE

Some say that sight begins to fade with age, requiring new prescription glasses, amended driver's licenses, and more squinting and focusing in order to distinguish what one is looking at. For South Carolina man Joseph Fuller, the evidence of his fading eyesight became clear when he picked up and drove off with a child he had mistakenly thought was his grandchild. Fuller didn't see his mistake until he returned home where hindsight is always twenty-twenty.

Being a helpful and under-occupied grandparent, Fuller agreed to pick his grandchild up after school one day, but it turns out that it would have helped if he knew what his grandchild looked like. Fuller showed up to Edisto Primary School in Orangeburg County, South Carolina, to pick up his grandson, watching all of the excited youth escape the mundane classroom for the day. He spotted who he believed was his grandson, walked up to the boy, gave him a hug, and asked if he was all ready to go. The boy agreed, and the two made their way back home.

It wasn't until Fuller returned to his house that he realized this child acted, sounded, and even looked different from what he remembered his grandson being like. Under a bit of anxiety and worry, Fuller knew he had the wrong kid and quickly went back to the school with the child. He apologized extensively and blamed it on geriatric confusion and the child's acquiescence to the situation.

Fuller was not the only one confused in the situation. It is reported that the teacher's assistant told sheriff's deputies that the little boy had said that Fuller was his grandfather, which allowed for the teacher to let the child go into Fuller's custody. The child even told Fuller that he was ready to go after he had given his mistaken grandfather a hug. Everyone seemed to be confused about who is family members with whom, but in the end, everything was straightened out with everyone safe at home.

## BROTHERS IN BROADCASTING
## CALLED OUT BY MOTHER

Brothers Dallas and Brad Woodhouse were opposing-viewpoint political commentators for C-SPAN, whose mother embarrassed them on-air as they argued over bipartisan politics in America. The two argued from opposite sides of the aisle, fighting with each other like they had since childhood. But even as the two men continued to butt heads into old age, their mother was still fed up with their combative relationship.

Point after point, the brothers had a queue of counter arguments lined up to one-up the other, turning their competitive childhood relationship into a successful broadcast television career. They received a call from a viewer, who was reportedly from "down south."

"You're right I'm from the south," the caller exclaimed as the brothers immediately realized who they were talking to. The sound of her on-air debut confirmed for the brothers that it was their mother on the line.

"Oh God, it's Mom," Dallas opined with embarrassment, slamming his face into his hands.

All the mother wanted was for her two sons to get along, but the broadcast was only breaking her heart more and more. Why did the brothers have to make a career out of arguing with each other? Is this what families do?

"No," she claimed, "not all families are like ours." Not all families argue on Thanksgiving and they especially don't argue on public television, but the Woodhouse family seems to be the exception.

The mother continued her call, saying that she was glad that the two of them were spending their Thanksgivings with their in-laws, because it might have provided some time for the two to get away from each other. That didn't happen. She only wished that by time Christmas came around that their bickering attitudes would recede. We're sure nothing changed between the brothers that holiday season, but let's hope that their argumentative nature will one day bring peace to Earth in the form of quality and informative news.

# EMBARRASSED ON THE JOB

*We all have our off days—it's understandable. But let's hope that someone isn't going to broadcast your most embarrassing mistakes when those days occur. Sometimes you can be overwhelmed, and you overlook something that shouldn't have been, or sometimes you're confused and are not sure how to act. You'd hope that the training for a new job would prepare you for all of those situations, but it can't. You have to remain on your toes if you are to keep your most embarrassing mistakes to yourself, but sometimes you can't. Sometimes things that you don't want to slip by do and end up gaining the attention of your peers.*

*Whatever happens, it's best to try to keep these slip-ups away from your boss. Who knows how they might react when you thought you sent a romantic email to your loved one, but ended up sending it to the one you despise most. Who knows how they might react when they see you walking out of the restroom with a trail of toilet paper following your every move. Keep alert. Try to watch yourself and your actions as carefully as you can, because you never know who might be watching.*

## THOUSANDS UNSURE ABOUT THEIR FUTURE

It can be incredibly exciting to receive a letter of acceptance from your first pick of colleges, and it can be incredibly devastating when you're denied. But what types of feelings are attached to an acceptance letter when you were not supposed to have received it. A notoriously nerve-racking experience for recent high-school graduates not only messes with the students' anxiety, but is now pulling at their heartstrings as well.

State University of New York at Buffalo sent out a few too many acceptance letters to its applicants recently, leading students on a roller-coaster of accomplishment and inadequacy. During an error that created a mistaken email list of accepted applicants, acceptance letters were sent out to 5,109 applicants who had actually been denied admission.

Prospective students' hearts soared and then plummeted as the university corrected their mistake with an email informing the ill-fated applicants that they had actually not been admitted. Although the whole process of applying to college can be daunting, it has now become a game for admission representatives who like to build up the hopes of the youth to only then break them down.

The University of Buffalo sent out their sincerest apologies to the students and their families, while also informing them to be sure to make other plans come the fall semester. Although some students still had the possibility of being accepted because they were still under review, the students had learned quickly that the lessons the institution had taught them were not to be trusted.

Other incidents of admission blunders from universities are not completely uncommon. Carnegie Mellon University and University of California at Los Angeles have also had hiccups in their admissions processes as well. While these schools only sent out acceptance letters to a few hundred rejected applicants before, the University of Buffalo now takes the prize with its thousands of disaffected prospective students.

## WELL-KNOWN SATELLITE MISTAKEN AS SOMETHING MYSTERIOUS

An unknown light source shining from the sky was reported by an officer in Worcestershire, England. The officer called in the mysterious sighting, asking for back up to help investigate. The unnamed officer said the light was coming from the sky with an unknown provenance. Was it a UFO? Was it a car's headlights reflecting off of something? Was it the sun's rays reflecting off of something? Turns out, it was the well-known phenomenon of the sun's light reflecting off of . . . the full moon.

The young officer—still new to the beat, and apparently the night sky as well—was suspicious of the light and thought that it might have been a car's headlights. But where, he wondered, was the car? He called in the activity and began to investigate the situation. Nothing seemed to add up and he couldn't find a lead to follow. After twenty minutes of searching for clues, he came to the embarrassing conclusion that what he was looking at was the moon.

Before other officers could arrive on the scene, the officer called his sergeant back to clarify that he had been a little confused by the situation. It wasn't an unknown light source but just a full moon! The sergeant giggled on the other side of the line, wondering if the officer was pulling his leg.

The officer wasn't kidding and was obviously a little embarrassed by his lack of experience with the moon. Although the moon wasn't charged, the officer did feel like he would be charged with extreme stupidity by his peers the next day and decided to not show up for duty. Good thing the moon began to wane the next day, causing less confusion about its voluminous presence.

## YEARBOOKS RECALL A HAUNTING PAST

High-school yearbooks have always been good at bringing back memories of the past, but they shouldn't necessarily bring back memories of tyrannical dictators who have sent the world to war. A yearbook produced for a high-school in Pennsylvania recently released some well-known quotes of Adolf Hitler, Joseph Stalin, and Islamic State leader Abu Bakr al-Baghdadi. Although the contents of the book were reviewed multiple times and the quotes did not seem to set off editorial alarms, the attributes of the quotes were overlooked in the editorial process.

Students could buy the books for $100, but what they received was more than what they paid for. Students picked quotes to go in the yearbook, and although most seemed to be pretty standard, there were a few that stuck out as unacceptable. Adolph Hitler was quoted with, "Words build bridges into unexplored regions." Abu Bakr al-Baghdadi with, "Be just; the unjust never prosper. Be valiant. Keep your word, even to your enemies." Joseph Stalin was quoted with maybe the most controversial statement, "Ideas are more powerful than guns. We would not let our enemies have guns, so why would we let them have ideas?"

These quotes—the last one especially—seemed to counter the whole philosophy of our public education system, but the district spokeswoman, Angela Yingling, didn't see the fault falling on the district. She claimed that it is the responsibility of the yearbook staff, its sponsor, and the school's administration to make sure nothing offensive is printed in the institution's annual publication. Nearly four hundred yearbooks were distributed to the students, but punitive measures were not centered around an individual. Refunds or stickers to cover the offensive attributions were provided for any families who were offended by the incident.

## FRANCE'S NEW TRAINS ARE TOO BIG TO BE USED

France was close to having a major internal transportation breakdown after they received new train cars that were too wide for the stations they would operate in. The country's main train company had recently ordered a whole new batch of modern train cars to upgrade their system, but what they didn't realize was that they had upgraded in size as well.

The National Society of French Railways spent £15 billion on the upgrade, hoping that their efficient system will continue to outdo other countries' railway systems, but maybe they got a little too confident. It wasn't until after the trains were delivered that the mishap was recognized. News spread through France's major media outlets, quickly causing an embarrassment for the administration of the National Society of French Railways.

The mix-up is said to have occurred when the dimensions of the train were given to the manufacturer before the actual order was placed, not considering the discrepancy in measurements between rebuilt stations and older stations. The gaps between the train and the platform in the older stations were much more narrow than the standards the new stations followed, making the trains too wide to actually fit in between the platforms.

The company only seemed to create more problems for itself by trying to preempt problems that come with a forty percent increase expected to happen over the next decade. Along with the tens of billions of euros the company already spent on new train cars, another £50 million is now being used to update the platforms of thousands of stations across the country. No one was fired in the mishap except for the outdated trains.

## PENTAGON OFFICIAL GOES ON THE OFFENSIVE

The Pentagon's top civilian affairs official Bryan Whitman was recently charged with stealing the license plate off of—what he thought was—an illegally-parked car of a nanny. After being a little more than frustrated with the street-parking situation in his D.C. area neighborhood, Whitman began his string of license plate thefts on the car of a nanny who—day after day—had visitor permits to park in the area.

Whitman did not think that a visitor permit was acceptable for multiple-day use, so he began his vigilante attacks by taking her license plates not once or twice, but three times. Along with taking her plates, Whitman also left notes that threatened to have the car towed and the residents' visitor-parking permits revoked. Whitman must have been in a rage as—day after day—he found the car "illegally" parked in his neighborhood, resorting to theft instead of an amicable conversation with his neighbors.

After the second time Whitman stole the plates, the residents who hired the nanny set up surveillance cameras to catch the thief. Little did they know that they were messing with a top official at the Pentagon. After catching Whitman on tape, the residents contacted the authorities, who attained a search warrant to bring him to justice. Whitman gave up the plates without a fight and settled with the prosecutors on a $1,000 restitution payment to the nanny, thirty-two hours of community service, and an order to stay away from the nanny, the residents, and the block they live on.

If Whitman can stay out of trouble for ten months, the charges will be dropped, but who knows where his anger will lead him. Reports state that there is no shortage of parking available in his neighborhood and that the nanny had every right to use a visitor pass. Maybe he should worry more about the defensive positions of the United States as opposed to taking the offensive over "illegally-parked" nannies.

## LYING TO THE FIGHTING IRISH

Days after he was hired as Notre Dame University's head football coach, George O'Leary resigned from his position due to exposed inaccuracies on his resume.

Claiming he was much more accomplished in academic and athletic fields than he really was, O'Leary said the misstatements were remnants from older resumes that "filled-out" his experience when he was still building his career.

After O'Leary was hired by the university, his employers began to fact check his credentials, finding that his supposed master's degree in education and experience playing college football were both fictitious. O'Leary claimed that he had received a master's degree in education from NYU-Stony Brook University—which is a faux conglomeration of two universities nearly fifty miles apart—and that he had also played on the University of New Hampshire's football team for three years as an undergraduate. The reality is that he attended two classes of his master's degree program before he dropped out, and that he had never set foot on the field for New Hampshire.

O'Leary expressed his deepest apologies for the shame and disrepute he brought to the Notre Dame legacy, but has continued making football history. Despite the inaccuracies on his resume, O'Leary had a successful career with the Georgia Tech Yellow Jackets from 1994 to 2001 and has since become the defensive coach for the Minnesota Vikings.

## DOES THIS NEWS HAVE A CREDIBLE SOURCE?

The *New York Times* found itself embarrassed when it published a fake article from reputable news comedians, *The Onion*. To commemorate the recently deceased

founder of *Tiger Beat* magazine, the *New York Times* published a gallery of covers of the magazine with one discrepancy in the mix: one of the covers was a fake.

The fake *Tiger Beat* cover featuring President Obama was made by *The Onion* to spoof the magazine and falsely claims that an early article by the tweeny-pop news source had contributed greatly to Obama's rise in popularity. It seems like some of the news world's most notorious fact checkers let this anomaly slip by them, giving credence to *The Onion*'s ability to spoof the news in a facsimile indistinguishable from reality.

## THE MAYOR'S BAG OF DIRTY TRICKS

The mayor of an upscale town in Southern California resigned after he was caught on tape messing with some dirty business. No, he wasn't caught having an affair or embezzling money or any of that dirty mayor stuff that happens regularly. He was filmed throwing a bag full of dog poo onto his neighbor's front porch.

Surveillance cameras on the San Marino home caught footage of the town's beloved mayor, Dennis Kneier, finding a bag of dog poo hung on a light-post, picking it up, and then flinging it into the residents' yard. After the homeowners found the footage, they originally didn't know that it was their mayor who was the offender, but authorities quickly identified the mayoral mischief-maker.

Sorry for his inappropriate misuse of refuse, Kneier publicly apologized to the residents, but they had a hard time getting over the offense. The resident claims that the mayor's action was not a mistake but retaliation in response to the resident opposing the mayor's plan for a city dog park. If so, this is the mayor's clear-cut message as to why there should be a dog park in the city.

Kneier's actions garnered national attention and enraged enough people to show up at the next city council meeting to call for Kneier's resignation. Kneier didn't put up a fight. He knew he should have left the bag where he had found it or thrown it away properly. Kneier claims that he will pay a littering fine and resign from his position as mayor, but he will remain a member of the city council. He now vouches that he will not let the city down by throwing anymore dog poo around.

## AIRLINE IS NOT SURE WHO THEY ARE APOLOGIZING TO, OR FOR WHAT

Customer service can make or break a relationship with an angered customer. They can apologize and cater to the customer's wants and needs in order to keep the customer loyal, happy, and willing to return, or they can totally miss the mark and lose the customer forever. One thing is for sure, you don't want to make the customer feel like just another person you have to deal with because it's your job, and at the very least, you'll need to know their name, their problem, and what they're talking about.

A recent incident a customer had with United Airlines is a great example of everything that customer service shouldn't do. The customer had encountered a problem with the airline and decided to contact customer service with her complaint, but what she received was not what she was looking for and did little to resolve her problem. The person whose job it is to fill the specific information into the apology-letter template failed, barely getting the customer's name in there just once (although it has been redacted here). Fed up with the lack of service, the customer decided to put the company on blast by posting it to Reddit. Here is what she received from the airline:

"Dear Mrs. [Redacted],

Thank you for letting us know about your recent experience with United Airlines. I apologize if our service did not meet your expectations, and appreciate you taking time to share your concerns.

Our goal is to provide a consistently reliable product and an exemplary level of customer service. Based on the events you describe, we did not meet this goal. Your comments regarding (SPECIFIC EVENT) will be used for coaching and training our employees.

To encourage you to fly with us again and as a tangible means of acknowledging your disappointment, enclosed is (SPECIFIC ITEM).

(CUSTOMER NAME), I ask that you allow us another

opportunity to serve you, as we consider it our privilege to have you aboard."

To make things worse, United Airlines heard news about their letter becoming popular on viral feeds, and claimed that they believe the letter is a fake. They just can't do anything right to make this situation better for themselves. One solution might be for United Airlines to just give up and let us all fly for free because everyone is fed up with the low quality and high price of air travel.

# CHAPTER 10:
# UNDER THE SUPERVISION OF BAD PARENTS

The line that defines bad parenting is subjective. You may think that your parents were bad parents because they worked too much or because they hovered over your every move, but these considerations have nothing on some of the bad parents that are out there. Some parents don't care, and some parents care too much. Either position can lead to what you may call "bad parenting." Parents may have the right intention or not, but what really matters is the example of adulthood they present to their children. If parents act like kids in front of their children, how will their children act when they reach adulthood? People learn from those who come before them, and if those who come before them have nothing to teach, then the children have nothing to learn.

Children are helpless under the supervision of their parents. They rely on their guardians to direct them towards clear definitions of what is right and what is wrong, but sometimes they never get a clear answer. Parents may say one thing but then contradict themselves with their actions. Parents may lead by example with all of the wrong actions. A clear definition of what is right and wrong is presented in the alignment of a parent's words and actions, but that rarely happens.

Parents aren't perfect, but they can sure be a lot better if they do the things they tell their children to do.

Some parents say all of the wrong things and some parents never say anything. Some parents do all the wrong things and others don't do anything at all. Children need to be guarded from the evils of the world, not exposed to them as their parents get by in the world by committing crimes. Children with bad parents are likely to learn how to be bad parents from them. What types of lessons do parents teach when they encourage their children to steal? What lessons are taught when parents trip on LSD in front of their kids? Hopefully, children are taking notes on what not to do instead of what they should do. You never know how you will influence a child, but bad parenting is a great way to insure that your child will encounter trouble in the future.

## PARENTS WHO CARE A LITTLE TOO LITTLE

*If you don't care enough for your child to strap them into their car seat or teach them that stealing is bad, then why did you have kids? If you don't care about kids, you shouldn't put yourself in the position to care for kids. Millions of kids aren't taught the valuable life lessons of what is right and wrong simply because their parents don't care if they learn the difference. Maybe their parents don't know the difference themselves.*

*Some parents have never grown up and never learn their lessons in life, while some kids have to grow up way too fast and quickly learn about the hardships of life. Whatever the dynamic of maturity is in a family, everyone should act their own age and be as mature as they can. No one wants to have to tell a kid to stop stealing watches from the nearby department store. No one wants to remind an adult that they should get a job and make a paycheck to support their family. But sometimes, reminders are needed in order to keep certain people on track.*

*Parents can care a lot, and they can not care at all. Who knows what makes the two, but both abound throughout the world. We're not sure what's worse, but parents who don't care enough seem to get in a little more trouble than those who do care. Some parents who don't care think their kids are little buddies that tag along with them wherever they go: their drug-dealer's house, a joy ride in a stolen car, a spree of thefts. Or they think their children are a burden and will only put in a minimum amount of effort to pacify their "needy" kids. Whatever they think, a good way to be a bad parent is to just not care.*

## WHAT A LONG AND STRANGE TRIP IT'S BEEN

A Michigan man, Phillip Englem, from Mukegon Charter Township, had a hell of a trip when he was arrested for shooting a gun at a local pizzeria while freaking out on LSD. Not only is that bad, but he was reportedly only wearing a towel and accompanied by his three children.

Engle, who lives next door to Happy's Pizza in Muskegon, is known to cause some trouble about town, but this incident definitely breaks all of his personal records. Wearing just a towel, Engle walked to the pizzeria with a gun in hand and began using the butt of the gun to bang on the glass entryway. The glass shattered and the gun then fell and discharged.

An employee at Happy's Pizza reports that Engle was screaming, "No one will help me! No one will feed my kids!" Then, followed by a deep moment of self-awareness, he muttered, "I'm tripping out."

It might seem funny, but the children were awfully scared. Police were called. They arrived at Engle's house where he sat on the porch with a handgun—supposedly a different gun than before. As ordered, he threw the gun into the front yard and then revealed that he had three more guns—that were loaded—inside the house.

While being interviewed, Engle revealed that he had ingested four hits of LSD earlier that day and that he had been having a rough trip. One of Engle's children told officers that he had also shot the dashboard of his car because it wouldn't stop beeping. They found a spent casing and a bullet hole to confirm the story.

Engle was arraigned on four misdemeanor charges: malicious destruction of property, careless discharge of a firearm, reckless use of a firearm, and possession of a firearm while under the influence. Engle will eventually be convicted for bad parenting.

## A DENVER WOMAN'S NIGHT OF FUN TURNS INTO A LIFETIME OF PAIN

A Denver, Colorado, woman got into a bit of trouble after she crashed her car, assaulted a police officer, and locked her eleven-month-old child alone in her apartment. The woman, Melissa Boyd, had gone out for a night of drinking, but before she left, she had to make sure her child was safe. She left the child behind in the apartment, which might have been a good thing because what she was about to get into was no scene a child should see.

Police were originally called to a hit-and-run accident scene which Boyd had caused and fled. But Boyd didn't get far before the cops pulled her over. Reports state that Boyd was loud and aggressive, lacking balance, and spoke with slurred speech—classic signs for a police officer to question whether she had been drinking that evening. Obviously, Boyd had few drinks that night, which was confirmed by the officer with a field sobriety and blood test.

Boyd had been in trouble before. Her record showed that she had been put on a restrained license after having a blood alcohol level of .08 in Vail years before. And she had been arrested for DUI twice before.

After busting Boyd for driving under the influence, investigators soon discovered her child left alone at home. And not only that, Boyd then kicked a sheriff's deputy in the throat while she was being medically examined at the Denver Health Medical Center.

The whole night totaled a whopping nine charges against Boyd, including second-degree assault, child abuse, driving under the influence, driving under restraint, lack of compulsory insurance, leaving the scene of an accident, and failure to report an accident. Boyd is being held with a $10,000 bond while her child is with Denver Protective Services.

## MOTHER AND DAUGHTER DUO NOT THE PERFECT TEAM

It's pretty bad when you get your eleven-year-old daughter to shoplift for you, but it's even worse when you ditch her after the cops pick her up. A mother from Troy, Michigan, allegedly convinced two children—one being her eleven-year-old daughter—and an older woman to help her shoplift from an Old Navy store in town. Her daughter was taken in by the police but the mother refused to pick her daughter up from jail that night.

The forty-nine-year-old woman had convinced her eleven-year-old daughter, a young boy, and a sixty-one-year-old woman to be accomplices in her Old Navy merchandise heist. The four entered the store around 8:00 p.m. and made their way to different departments to begin stuffing merchandise into various bags. Security cameras caught all of the action, while the security guards were only able to catch the eleven-year-old daughter and the sixty-one-year-old woman. The mother of the daughter and the young boy were able to get away before the police arrived.

The eleven-year-old was found with $123.95 worth of stolen baby clothes, jewelry, and women's shirts. She told investigators that her mother had instructed her to steal the items and then meet her back by the car, but she never made it to the parking lot. Instead, she made it to the local police station.

Authorities later called the mother to come and pick her child up, but she—in a paranoid manner—denied that she had been at the store earlier, claiming she knew nothing of the incident. She said she would not be picking up her daughter. The Michigan woman then called a few hours later to admit that she lied about the situation because she was scared, so scared that she still never came to pick up her daughter. An aunt came to pick the child up later that night, and the mother is now wanted for retail fraud, child neglect, and contributing to the delinquency of a minor.

## THIS IS NO LIVING SITUATION FOR CHILDREN

Police in South Carolina walked into a disaster zone as they responded to a call in a residential area of the city. Police found the living conditions abhorrent and three children—ages eight, nine, and ten—living in the mess.

The mother of the children, Alison Alsbrooks Scurry, had been overwhelmed with the daunting task of being a single parent and began to let household tasks fall by the wayside. Police found nearly a foot of trash—including rotting food—covering the floors of the entire house.

Scurry was charged with unlawful conduct toward a child and was encouraged to clean up her act before more severe punitive measures came down on her.

## CHILDREN REPLACED WITH GAS CANS

Colorado resident, Sandra Ramirez, was outed as a bad parent after local media caught up to her about a photo circulating the internet. Apparently, the Colorado Department of Transportation recently posted a photo onto their Facebook page of a young child and gas can sharing the backseat of a car, except the can was strapped into the child seat while the child freely roamed.

After so much buzz stirred around the photo, media officials decided to investigate the case and find the owner and mother of the car and child. They eventually caught up with Sandra Ramirez for an explanation.

"I'm not a bad mom," she claims, "I'd just like to clarify that."

Kids can be a handful, but this seems like something that could have been prevented by not putting the gas can where the child goes. She claims that her son is a very smart boy, and that he undoes his seatbelt all the time. That can understandably happen, but does the child then put the gas can in his place? How things actually happened are still unclear, but Ramirez is due to appear in court to help clarify the situation.

## CARS, CHILDREN, AND STRIP CLUBS DON'T MIX

A twenty-four-year-old woman, Kelsey McMurty, was charged with child neglect, criminal impersonation, and driving without a license. She was busted for leaving her thirteen-month-old child in the car as she auditioned as a dancer at a gentleman's club in Nashville, Tennessee.

According to the police report, McMurty left her child in the car with a friend who was supposed to be watching the child as she auditioned for the job. The only thing is, her friend, Summer Taylor, didn't watch the child but, instead, went into the club to watch McMurty's audition.

Officers were called onto the scene after they received a call of the child left alone in the car. The windows were all the way up in the car and the child was wearing a thick winter jacket, which led the officers to worry. The infant was covered in sweat after spending thirty minutes in the car. The officer reported that it was 72 degrees outside and most likely near 100 degrees within the car.

The child was taken to the hospital for treatment, while the Department of Children's Services was called to tend to the child and to the scene of the incident. Both McMurty and Taylor were booked with child neglect and given respective $40,000 and $10,000 bonds.

## COME ON KIDS WE'RE GOING FOR A BEER RUN

When you say, "buckle up," in Australia, it doesn't refer to making sure you're safe while in the car, it means making sure the beer is safe while in the car. A Broome, Australia, man was recently pulled over on the Great Northern Highway of Australia. Police found the driver to have multiple cases of beer secured with the seatbelts in the backseat, while children were found sitting freely in the foot wells behind the seats.

Police say that several children, including a child of less than a year old, were lying on the laps of adults in the car and pretty much everywhere but the seats, as cases of beer were piled in the backseat and strapped in.

The man driving was a suspended driver and was charged with no authority to drive and failure to restrain a child. Police in the area say that they are not surprised by the incident, and that it seems to reflect the priorities people have while using the roadways of Australia.

Multiple stops have occurred in the area finding large amounts of alcohol being illegally transported to aboriginal lands. Reports of suspended drivers on the road are even more common. Authorities are trying to stamp these problems out by creating education programs to bring awareness to the rural folks of the Outback.

## FATHER OF A DAUGHTER HAS
## NO RESPECT FOR WOMEN

A father from Van Nuys, California, obviously had other things on his mind when he left his nine-month-old daughter unattended in a locked car for an hour. He needed some time away from the family and went into a strip club for a few lap dances.

Twenty-four-year-old, Auwin Dargin, has been charged with child abuse after leaving his infant daughter in the car as he visited Synn Gentleman's Club in North Hills, California. Suspicion began as the assistant manager of the strip club, Matthew Nadeau, began to notice Dargin leaving the club every fifteen minutes and then returning. Nadeau then began to search the parking lot, heard crying coming from a car, and came across Dargin's car with Dargin's daughter still in the back.

A waitress at the club and Nadeau rescued the child with the help of other business owners in the area by pushing down the open window in the back seat. They connected the dots and realized that the child was Dargin's, who was receiving a lap dance inside of the club at the time. They interrupted the dance to inform Dargin that they had saved his child and that the authorities were on their way.

Dargin is reported to have said, "Just give me my baby and I know I'm messing up." But the baby was not returned to him. Nadeau and the staff of Synn Gentleman's Club prevented Dargin from leaving before he was met by law enforcement. The child was taken into Child Protective Services and later released to her mother, while Dargin awaits his verdict. If he is found guilty of child abuse, he faces up to six years in jail.

## NINE-YEAR-OLD LIVING IN THE MOTOR CITY KNOWS HOW TO DRIVE

A man from Detroit, Michigan, Shawn Weimer, is facing felony charges of second-degree child abuse for allowing his nine-year-old daughter to act as his designated driver at 3:00 a.m. The judge has not yet decided whether the charges will be seen as a felony or misdemeanor because no one was hurt. Plus, his daughter's driving skills were impeccable.

The incident was likely to cause physical harm to someone, but it didn't. Weimer's daughter claims that her father finished half of a bottle of Black Velvet and threw the rest out before they started making their way home.

Although Weimer was drunk, his daughter followed every rule of the road, using her turn signals, stopping at stops signs and red lights, and keeping her speed within the legal limit. She was obviously surprised when she was pulled over that night because she had done nothing wrong.

The defense argued that the girl was an experienced driver because she was familiar with driving ATVs and dirt bikes. They also argued that because no one was hurt, the charges should be seen as a misdemeanor and not a felony. No matter what the decision, it's agreed that the girl is a good driver, and the father is a bad parent.

UNDER THE SUPERVISION OF BAD PARENTS

# TEN-YEAR-OLD GETS HIS FIRST TATTOO

A Georgia mother has been arrested for allowing her ten-year-old son to get a memorial tattoo of his deceased brother's name. She claimed she didn't know it was illegal even if she gave consent. The mother, Chuntera Napier, was touched when her son, Gaquan, asked about getting a tattoo for his brother, who had died recently from being hit by a car. She couldn't say no, and she claimed it actually made her feel good that he cared so much.

The two of them both received tattoos of their deceased loved-one's name and his basketball-jersey number on their right arms. Authorities at Gaquan's school noticed the tattoo and called the police, who arrested Chuntera later that day.

She claims, "I always thought that if a parent gave consent, then it was fine. How can somebody else say that it's not okay? He's my child, and I have the right to say what I want for my child. I can't go tell anybody else what I want for their child."

Although it may seem like the state is impinging on her duties and responsibilities as a parent, the law clearly states, "It shall be unlawful for any person to tattoo the body of any person under the age of eighteen, except a physician or osteopath."

Not only is Napier in trouble for allowing her son to get a tattoo, but the tattoo artist can be charged as well. Napier would not reveal who the artist was, but authorities expect that the tattoos were done in an illegal situation operating without a license.

## PARENTS FAIL TO KEEP DRUGS AWAY FROM CHILD

Alysia Lombard and Mario Hollerway, parents of a three-year-old child, have been charged after their child was hospitalized and tested positive for THC.

That night Lombard had fed the girl some food and started a movie before she had to go to work. Everything seemed fine, and she continued on her way. As she arrived to work, she received a call from Hollerway saying that their child wasn't acting right. He took her to Rose Medical Center in Denver, Colorado, where she immediately threw up.

Although the girl was not injured, she did ingest marijuana, which caused her nauseating side effects. Investigators found that Lombard and Hollerway had expired red cards—a medical marijuana license—and had begun their own homegrown operation well within the legal limits of Colorado law. A can of cannabutter was also found in the house. The night of the incident, police found a plastic container containing 8.8 ounces of marijuana with an open lid on top of Lombard and Hollerway's bed.

Maybe a little anxious about the cops in his house, Hollerway also admitted to having a "T-shirt of dope behind the TV." The dope that he was referring to was crack cocaine.

Investigators also noted the household was no place for a child. There was debris on the floor throughout the house, garbage within reach of children, trash bags lying on the floor of the child's room, and many other messes that were not suitable for children to live around.

Hollerway was eventually charged with possession of a controlled substance, misdemeanor possession of six to twelve ounces of marijuana, and misdemeanor child abuse. Lombard was charged with the latter two. Hollerway was given two years in prison, while Lombard will be serving an eighteen-month probation as well as attending drug treatment sessions and parenting classes.

## GIRL LEFT ALONE IN THE DESERT WITH LOADED GUN

An Arizona man is facing child endangerment charges after he left his five-year-old granddaughter alone in the desert with a .45-caliber—cocked and loaded—handgun. What began as a wholesome ride in grandpa's pickup truck turned into a near death situation for the little girl.

As the two drove through the desert, they came across a stretch of road they couldn't pass and got stuck. Having forgotten his cellphone that day, the grandfather, Paul Rater, thought it was best to walk for help. His granddaughter didn't last long under the beating sun, so he left her under a tree with a loaded gun just in case she encountered any "bad guys."

Rater continued on his way to get help, which was apparently a few drinks and a cheeseburger in his mind.

Rater came across many people as he made it back to town, but it never occurred to him to try to use their cellphones to call for help. He kept going, but not before he told those he encountered that he left his granddaughter in the desert, and that they should keep an eye out for her.

He made a few more stops on his way. Witnesses at the South Buckeye Equestrian Center claim that Rater came through at about 5:30 p.m. complaining about the ten-mile walk, but he never mentioned his granddaughter. His wife reports that she received a call from Rater an hour later asking for a ride from the local burger joint.

An off-duty fireman riding his ATV in the desert eventually found the little girl. Notoriously repugnant Sheriff Joe Arpaio showed a bit of his nice side as he commented on the situation, "He told her [the gun] was to shoot bad guys. How does a five-year-old know the difference between good guys and bad guys?" Obviously, Arizonans are not sure why you shouldn't leave kids with guns, but they sure know that you're not supposed to leave a child in the desert for too long. Rater is being held on a $25,000 bond and is being charged with child abuse.

## CHILDREN FOUND LIVING IN ABANDONED BUS

Two children were found outside of the Houston area of Texas living in a bus all by themselves. They are now in the custody of child welfare authorities, but what happened to their parents?

Reports say that the two children continued to live in the bus they had been living in with their father and mother before their parents were arrested for embezzlement. The mother, Sherrie Shorten, tried to explain that the bus was only a temporary housing situation after they moved out of their apartment when funds were low.

But things never got better. The parents were arrested and the children were—ostensibly—forgotten about. No one reported the children being  alone because they were in the middle of the forest and neither of them were enrolled in local school. We're not sure how the parents were arrested without the kids being known about, but the kids continued tending to their business.

They were home schooled, so they kept in touch with their mother in jail to receive lesson plans. They called their mother if they had any questions about exponents or other math related topics. Unfortunately, the children had not yet been taught how to take care of themselves. Shorten wants to live with her children again once she gets out of jail, but Child Protective Services are wary of the lessons she might teach them.

# PARENTS WHO CARE A LITTLE TOO MUCH

*Not only is not caring a good way to be a bad parent, but even caring too much can lead to some bad parenting techniques. Some parents care so much that the little things that "disenfranchise" their child from the same opportunities as other children will lead them to act erratically. They can explode at any minute if they think their child is being taken advantage of.*

*Everyone cares about something, but those cares usually shift when you have children. All the friends, hobbies, and activities you once enjoyed may fall to the wayside when a child comes into your life. You can't help but to want the best for your child and be willing to die to attain it for them. You can't help but to fight tooth and nail for the most popular toy of the season before it sells out. Parents will go to the ends of the world to give their children what they need, but, sometimes, parents think that their children need more than they actually do.*

*It is a good thing to want the best for your child, but you should realize that the best might not be worth it if you have to stoop down low to get it. You must choose your battles because not all of them are worth fighting. If you care too much, you may find yourself fighting for the silliest of reasons, teaching your child some lessons that are better left untaught. Don't get us wrong, it's good to care, but you must realize that it's your child you should care for and not where your child stands in relation to their peers. Take a step back, get out of the helicopter, and let the child learn their own lessons for once.*

## FRONT ROW SEATS HAVE A HIGH PRICE TO PAY

A crowd of nearly three hundred parents attending their kindergartners' school play broke out in pandemonium after fights over seating erupted. The Ridgemoor Elementary students of Manifee, California, were obviously nervous about their onstage debut because their parents had such high expectations. The parents waited patiently in the auditorium with white knuckles. They wanted their children to shine, but the friction between parents would eventually cancel the show.

Like usual, some parents showed up early to grab the front-row seats while the latecomers were left with the seating they could find. Towards the front, parents began setting up their video cameras to film their young stars, but the parents up front weren't having it.

Arguments between the parents in the front row and the filming parents broke out, and one thing led to another—like usual—from verbal attacks to punches being thrown.

Police were called to the scene to deal with the hundreds-strong crowd in tumult. The play was canceled. No one was arrested that night, but punitive measures were drawn out by the brawlers' spouses.

## MOTHER BARELY SAVES BABY

Tiffany Lawson, a resident of Cleveland, Ohio, came home to a situation that no one wants to find themselves in. Her baby-daddy, Kevin Ford Jr., was in a fit of rage, and she knew his fits led to homicidal tendencies. The situation was not safe. Ford crashed through the house in anger, yelling and smashing belongings, and then—unbelievably—covered Lawson and their son, Kevin Ford III, in lighter fluid.

Lawson had to think quickly. She knew that if her son were to stay in the room that he would be badly burnt, if not killed. So she did what she thought was best to protect her son: threw him out the window.

Ford III fell two stories out the window, but somehow the child was able to land safely from the fall. And it wasn't that the child was just lucky enough to not be injured from hitting the ground, he was so lucky that someone actually saw him falling and caught him.

Tiffany Lawson was not as lucky as her son. Immediately after she threw her son out the window, psychotic Ford Jr. then lit Lawson on fire. She then threw herself out of the window—breaking her arm and elbow—to then rip off her burning clothes.

Lawson was hospitalized to treat her breaks and the burns she sustained on her hands and legs. Kevin Ford Jr. was arrested for attempted murder and booked in jail. When asked about the situation, he responded to the police, "I just lost my temper."

## PARENT KIDNAPS THEIR OWN CHILD

Tiffany Rasnic recently updated her Facebook relationship status to "divorced." There had been trouble at home, but the subsequent posts seemed to show that Rasnic was doing well. She had gotten back on her feet, got a new place, and bought a new SUV. But she would end up arrested a few days later for trying to get what she really needed: her son.

On October 26, 2015, a relative went to her son's school and picked the boy up. At an intersection, there was some type of hand off of the child from one car to another. A white SUV pulled up to the relative's car, flashed a badge, and removed the child from the car to then speed off with him. Reports are unclear about this situation and what exactly happened, but an Amber Alert was issued soon afterwards.

Later, the boy was found at home with Rasnic, who was then arrested for kidnapping her son because she did not have parental custody of the child. No current charges are being held against her, but the identity of the man in the white SUV is still under investigation.

## NOSEY NEIGHBORS ARE A LITTLE PARANOID

A Canadian woman from British Columbia has been fined $65,000 for making unfounded accusations on social media. What were these accusations? She claimed that her neighbor was a pedophile.

The woman, Katherine Van Nes, believed that through a system of mirrors and cameras, her neighbor, Douglas Pritchard, was spying on her children when they played in the back yard. Her claims were not harmless; the judge ruled that her unsupported beliefs have had detrimental effects on her neighbor's social reputation and career as a middle-school music teacher.

Investigations into the situation show that the relationship between the neighbors began to deteriorate when Pritchard approached the Van Nes family about their new fountain. The fountain kept his wife from sleeping and he asked if they could turn it off at night. Pritchard's efforts for some peace and quiet, along with the installation of a decorative mirror in his backyard, led Van Nes to begin "venting" on social media about her neighbor.

The posts supposedly claimed that Pritchard may have had pedophilic tendencies and that he was a threat to the community—the worst blow a school teacher's reputation can receive. Although Van Nes deleted her posts within twenty-seven hours of putting them up, the damage had already been done.

Pritchard was awarded $50,000 in general damages, $15,000 in punitive damages, and $2,500 for his nuisance claim about the fountain. Not only that, but his original complaint was finally dealt with, and the Van Nes family was ordered to turn off their fountain between the hours of 10:00 p.m. and 7:00 a.m.

## TOO YOUNG TO DRIVE IN OHIO

A twenty-three-year-old Ohio man, Jaron Mcgee, trusted his nine-year-old daughter a little too much before they crashed into a tree. A little before the legal age-limit to start learning to drive, McGee thought it might be a good idea to give his daughter a head start with her driving lessons.

While visiting Headlands State Park, McGee placed his daughter in the driving seat and had her navigate the parking lot. He gave your standard tips for driving as she tried to look over the steering wheel: not too much gas, look both ways, and watch out for that tree.

But, as you would expect, the driving lesson didn't go as planned. The little girl lost control of the car and crashed into a tree on the edge of the lot. Family members were able to get the girl out of the car before authorities arrived, but onlookers were able to connect the chain of events that led to the crash.

McGee was charged with child endangerment and wrongful entrustment, while his daughter remains suspended from receiving her license for another seven years.

### MOTHER AND DAUGHTER
### LIKE TO PARTY TOGETHER

A mother from England, Nicola Austen, went too far when it came to planning her soon to be eighteen-year-old daughter's birthday party. Austen had invited all of her daughter's friends, rented a limo to take them to London, and bought twelve bags of cocaine—weighing 8.65 grams—in order to insure that she, her daughter, and all of the partygoers had a good time.

The day before the party, Austen had a bit of bad luck when police came by to question her, halting her plans for the narcotics ridden party. Austen had several counts on her record already, including methamphetamine possession, which led to the police showing up that day. But the police didn't come alone; they had a drug-sniffing dog with them that picked up on the scent of narcotics.

Austen admitted to possessing cocaine and that it was for her daughter's birthday party. All they wanted was to have a good time, but no fun was had. Austen was made to serve a nine-month suspension and unpaid work time instead of jail time. The judge decided not to jail her because she had a young son who would suffer if Austen were incarcerated.

## AFTER-SCHOOL BRAWL IN TEXAS GOES TOO FAR

Local Texan mother Viridiana Alvarez was arrested recently for helping her daughter out in a schoolyard scuffle. She didn't pull some hair or surreptitiously trip a child, but something much worse: she pulled a gun on the girl her daughter was fighting.

Alvarez was charged with aggravated assault with a deadly weapon after the photo of the ridiculous situation surfaced online. The photo shows Alvarez pointing the gun at the head of her daughter's rival as a group of girls stand around recording the fight with their smartphones.

The fight was obviously the talk of the town. Both of the girls' parents knew about the fight, but only one parental unit decided to step into the situation. The father of the girl who was assaulted by Alvarez said he knew about the fight, but only became worried when he saw the photos.

It was an everyday after-school fight over a boy, but it ended up having larger repercussions than whom Johnny would decide to go to the dance with. Alvarez was detained by police and held in Harris County Jail on a $35,000 bond.

## MOTHER BURNS HER CHILDREN'S MATTRESSES AND SHOOTS THEIR PHONES

A local Georgia mother has come to face some dire consequences for the video of her shooting her children's cellphones she posted online. Deborah Smith, of Coweta County, gained the media's attention and much more with her aggressive parenting techniques.

Parents around the internet both applauded and criticized Smith's practices, but she claims that her discipline worked for a little while. She had recently had problems with her two teenage sons, Ethan and Robbie, who were beginning to cause trouble by staying out all night, doing and selling drugs, and sleeping all day. In order to deal with their increasing delinquency, she turned to extreme measures.

"Today, we're going to take that option of where to sleep away," Smith exclaims in her video as the camera pans to show the boys' mattresses burning in the yard. "Boys, this is all that's left of your beds. I'm sorry, but they exploded," she explains. Smith then cocks her rifle and shoots at their cellphones smoldering in the fire.

Although some other locals thought it was the right measure to take, a viewer forwarded the video to Coweta County Department of Children and Family Services who began their investigation. After compromising with Smith to sign a safety plan to not use her firearms in front of her children, DCFS had to remove her two teenage sons from her custody.

Although Smith could have kept her boys if she agreed to a firearm safety plan, she refused to cooperate because she believed it impeded her from using her First and Second Amendment Rights. She didn't know what else to do.

"They're at the cusp of being seventeen years old, where it goes from being juvenile offenses to adult offenses. I just don't know where it's going to end. I don't want them to die," she laments.

Although she admits that she did burn their mattresses and shot-up their phones, she claims she did it because she wanted to catch the attention of her children before it was too late for them to learn responsibility.

## EASTER EGG HUNT TURNS INTO A STAMPEDE

The PEZ Candy company abruptly stopped their annual Easter egg hunt in Orange, Connecticut, because parents turned the childhood tradition into a mess of an argument.

Each year, 9,000 eggs are scattered throughout three fields—each field for different age groups—for the children to run around and collect. Every fifteen minutes, children  are released into the field, but impatient parents began rushing the field anyways.

Spectators claimed that the hordes of parents trampled a few children, separated some from their parents, and even gave one child a bloody nose as he was pushed over. Many blamed the PEZ Candy company for the upheaval, but PEZ responded on their website by saying, "Grow up folks and teach your kids some responsibility by acting like mature adults, not rabid dogs."

Some commenters believe the parents were greedy and aggressive just because they wanted the most eggs. Talks of next year's Easter egg hunt are underway, but they are not sure if they'll need security guards or not.

## WHEN GOOD PARKING IS LIKE GOLD

It's only a matter of time before people lose their minds over the lack of parking that is available. Multiple women were filmed in the Houston Zoo's parking lot brawling over a parking spot.

A video posted online of the incident reached nearly one hundred thousand views in just one day. Some viewers lamented about how the adults can behave like children, but most agreed that there is a lack of parking at the park.

The video shows many women fighting and throwing punches over a parking spot that one of the women was saving for her family—apparently this is not the etiquette to follow when saving a parking space.

At one point, a woman with a stroller comes in the frame and joins in on the brawl with her child watching her. Reports are not sure if the woman and her child had any stake claimed in the parking spot, but she sure came in with her fists flying.

# CHAPTER 11:
# JUST PLAIN STUPID PT. 2

No matter how well humans have climbed to the top of the food chain and totally kicked butt at the game of evolution, they are still not perfect. Everyday they get better and better, learning from their mistakes and adapting to this fickle and dynamic world. It's a slow process though. It takes time to reflect on one's actions and realize where mistakes were made. It takes time to change one's behavior and to act according to the situation.

There are those people who want to adapt and learn, and then there are those who really don't care about correcting their behavior. They will act the way they want to and if people think it's stupid, then so be it. Some people may genuinely not care if you think they're stupid, and others just don't realize that they're stupid. Stupid is stupid and there is no getting around it. This last chapter only has the theme of "stupid," there are no sub-themes or categories for them to fall in to; it's all just plain stupid.

Maybe try to learn something from this book or just use it as entertainment, but remember you're a local as well. You are just as likely to find yourself at the center of the headlines for the embarrassing situations you may find yourself in. No one is exempt from scrutiny, so keep yourself prepared for anything.

## LOCALS WORRY ABOUT
## THE NINJAS IN THE WOODS

In 2008, schools in Barnegat, New Jersey, were put on lockdown. The reason? Someone spotted a stealthy ninja, dressed in black and carrying a sword, running through the woods behind an elementary school.

The "ninja" turned out to be a camp counselor who was late to a costume-themed event at the local middle school. His black outfit was a karate uniform, and his threatening sword was made of plastic. When it comes to ninjas, it's better to be safe than sorry!

## LOCAL SAVES MONEY ON GAS

Apparently, Daniel C. Guthrie of West Fargo, North Dakota, likes to push his luck. Guthrie is facing charges for driving off from a gas station without paying. But not just once or twice—he went to the same station thirteen times before he was finally arrested.

Between April and May of 2016, Guthrie repeatedly visited the Little Duke's station in Fargo. The smallest charge he skipped out on was $11.25, and the largest was $29.01.

He faces thirteen counts of theft. According to City Attorney Erik Johnson, all of the drive-offs were documented by surveillance footage.

## MCDONALD'S IS FINALLY
## GIVING BACK TO THE COMMUNITY

Some people are wary of eating at McDonald's because there have been questions about what goes into their food. But Dave Cook, of Chesterfield County, Virginia, found something in his burger that was worth the visit to the fast food establishment. Cook found a $20 bill sandwiched between two pieces of meat on his sandwich.

Cook, who stopped at the restaurant with his mom for a quick bite to eat, was shocked when he found the money hanging from his mouth.

"I've heard of people finding strange things in their salad, but never finding something like this in a cooked burger," he said. "I was in disbelief; I was like 'is this for real?'"

Other patrons began searching for money in their meals, as well, but unfortunately, it doesn't look like McDonald's has started cooking with cash. The managers of the McDonald's have no idea how the money wound up in the burger and have referred the incident to their corporate office.

## EATING WHILE DRIVING IS FOUND TO BE JUST AS DISTRACTING AS TEXTING

Anthony Magga, of Petaluma, California, proved why it's not always safe to eat and drive. The pickup driver was attempting to unwrap a sandwich while he was behind the wheel of his truck when he lost control and clipped the side-view mirror of an oncoming motorcycle, according to California Highway Patrol officials.

The motorcycle riders—David McLean and his wife, Nancy, both of Petaluma—were taken to Santa Rosa Memorial Hospital with moderate-to-minor injuries.

California Highway Patrol officers determined that Magga was distracted by his sandwich, which resulted in the accident.

## STUDENT TURNS INTO INDECENT TRASH MAN

In case you need more examples to prove why taking drugs is a bad idea, here's the story of Benjamin Abele. The University of Georgia student took PCP one night in May 2016, and then proceeded to dive naked into a garbage truck.

A police officer saw Abele running naked toward the truck, which was stopped during its usual route at about 2:30 a.m. Abele then hopped right into the "dirty and foul liquid" in the back of the truck, and the officer found the student curled up in the trash with "a dazed look on his face," according to reports.

When the officer attempted to pull Abele from the trash, the student became combative, burrowing deeper into the trash while punching and kicking the officer. Eventually, Abele was struck with a Taser, which had little effect on the PCP-addled man. It took four police officers to finally subdue Abele.

He was charged with felony obstruction and public indecency and released on bond, jail records show.

Abele, a senior in management information systems, recently won a $10,000 prize during the school's entrepreneurship competition for designing an ecommerce startup for art sales. Hopefully he learned his lesson and will steer clear of PCP and garbage trucks from now on!

## APARTMENT BUILDING WANTS TO BE FRIENDS WITH ITS RESIDENTS

The owners of an apartment building in Salt Lake City, Utah, recently forced its tenants to "friend" the building's page on Facebook, even going so far as to threaten to break their leases if they refused.

Residents of the City Park Apartments found a piece of paper stuck to their doors titled "Facebook Addendum." It stated that the residents had five days to connect with the City Park Apartment page on Facebook, or they'd be in breach of their lease, even if they'd signed their lease months earlier.

The addendum also stipulated that the building's owners could post pictures of tenants and their visitors to the Facebook page, and it required that tenants not post anything negative about the apartment complex.

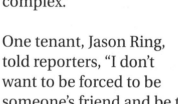

One tenant, Jason Ring, told reporters, "I don't want to be forced to be someone's friend and be threatened to break my lease because of that."

Ring believes, as no doubt many residents do, that it's a violation of his privacy. Kirk A. Cullimore, a lawyer for the firm which represents the building owners, offered this explanation:

"As part of opening its pool and an anticipated pool party, City Park desired to provide some protection to its residents and its owners from usage of photos on its Facebook page from all community events, including the opening pool party. The 'Facebook' addendum was provided to them to assist in that protection. That addendum went beyond the request and intent of City Park Apartments, and was not carefully reviewed to ensure that it met with their needs and requests. At no time was any resident in jeopardy of eviction or action from City Park for failure to sign the addendum or 'friend'

City Park Apartments. City Park has not implemented the addendum nor is it requiring its residents to execute it."

As of May 2016, the apartment complex had a 1.1-star rating on its Facebook page.

## WHY DO SOME PEOPLE HAVE CHILDREN?

Some people definitely shouldn't have children. Like Ashley Harmon and Jonathan Flint, of Layland, West Virginia. In June 2016, the couple took Harmon's three-month-old baby to a neighbor, Carolyn Redden, and asked her if she'd like to buy the child for between $500 and $1,000.

Redden of course refused, but seeing that the baby was in such poor hands, she took the baby to care for, and called 911 to report the couple.

"Why have a child if you're not going to care for it?" Redden said. "Just because it is hard doesn't mean you give up on a child."

Redden gave Harmon's and Flint's names and descriptions to detectives, and authorities were able to track them down and arrest them.

Redden's granddaughter, Tonya Kessler, said that the baby ended up in the right place.

"My grandma would do anything for anyone," Kessler said. "She is incredible. My question is, why are people like this having children? There are so many people who would love to have a baby and can't. I knew that baby was in the right hands when my grandma had her. She was well taken care of."

Child Protective Services will determine if the biological father of the child will be given custody.

## SPIDERMAN'S SPIDEY SENSES TINGLE AFTER A FEW DRINKS

A man in Torquay, England, got very drunk and decided to climb a cliff face, calling himself Spiderman. But after he'd climbed about sixty-five feet up the cliff, he got stuck.

Firefighters from Torquay fire station arrived on the scene, along with a specialty cliff rescue team from Plymouth.

A spokesman for the fire department said, "We were called out about 7:30 p.m. to a man who was very drunk. He had climbed up the cliff face from the bottom and was being very aggressive and very difficult. He was throwing things down towards the police. He was telling everyone he was Spiderman but he was very much in a position of quite big danger."

The firefighters were able to reach the man with specialist line equipment, and he was taken to an ambulance for care.

## CONFUSED MAN THINKS HE'S BEEN SHOT

A man in Texas called police to report that he'd been shot. But it turns out he was just bitten by his dog.

The man had been smoking marijuana on his porch as a thunderstorm passed through the area. Apparently a clap of thunder startled one of his dogs, which then nipped the man in his buttock. The alarmed man then called the police to report the "shooting."

An officer from the Groesbeck Police Department, near Waco, responded and discovered the man had been smoking marijuana and the "shooting" was simply a dog bite.

"During the course of the investigation, it was determined that the 'victim' had been smoking marijuana on the porch as the thunderstorm passed through the area," Groesbeck Police Chief Chris Henson said in a Facebook post. "The loud thunder scared one of the dogs causing it to nip the 'victim' in the left buttock. He believed he'd been shot and subsequently called the police."

Henson posted about the incident on Facebook because there had been rumors of a shooting in the area. The dog bite victim was treated at the scene and released.

## ONE-ARMED BANDIT BRAWLS WITH A BOXER

A one-armed burglar attempted to rob a home in Florida one afternoon, but didn't realize that the homeowner was a Crossfit coach and boxer.

Albert Thompson broke into a home in Santa Rosa Beach when the homeowner was asleep, attempting to steal $80. But when the woman awoke to find him in her home, she was able to subdue him and keep him at the scene until police arrived.

While the fact that Thompson only has one arm may have given him less of an advantage, it's never a good idea to challenge someone who is used to lifting weights and throwing hooks and jabs.

Thompson was arrested and charged with burglary of an occupied dwelling, misdemeanor petit theft, and obstruction by a disguised person.

## HERE'S A TIP: DON'T OVER TIP

A man in Edgewater, Colorado, left an extra-generous tip at a restaurant, only to return the next day and ask for his money back.

Waiters at Thailicious were amazed when a diner left a $1,000 tip on a $40 bill.

Owner Nithiwadee Anantatho said that the highest tip they'd ever gotten previously was $100, so everyone was shocked by the high amount.

"We were like, 'Oh really? He must be a millionaire!'" Anantatho said.

But the truth was much more mundane: he was drunk.

And when he realized that he'd accidentally tipped the large amount of money, he returned, presumably quite sheepishly, to ask for the return of his money.

Despite having to give the money back, the staff at Thailicious continue to laugh about the man's mistake.

"It is just the way it is," Anantatho said.

After the restaurant returned the money, the patron gave them a still-respectable $50 tip.

### BETTER THAN NINE INCH NAILS

A twenty-eight-year-old man from Xinjiang, China, swallowed eight six-inch nails in an attempt to impress his friends. Not surprisingly, he was later rushed to the hospital.

According to Chinese media, the man swallowed the nails in March 2016, but he didn't report feeling any pain until two months later.

The man had first tried to convince his friends that he was a sword swallower, but they expressed their doubts about his story. Apparently lacking swords, the man produced a package of nails and began swallowing them. His friends finally stopped him after the eighth nail, fearing for his safety.

Doctors ordered an x-ray, which showed that several of the nails had pierced his stomach, and he was sent for emergency surgery.

"After swallowing the nails I didn't feel any pain. I didn't think anything of it. I never expected it would turn out so bad," said the man.

## RUNNING AWAY FROM COPS ISN'T A GOOD IDEA, ESPECIALLY WHEN THEY'RE TRYING TO HELP

A woman from Voorheesville, New York, crashed her car against a guardrail, asked for help from a nearby resident, and then ran away and fell off a cliff.

According to a witness, Erika A. Barkman had been driving erratically before crashing her car. She then went to the home of a nearby resident and asked for help, saying she was being "chased by cops." The resident stated that Barkman smelled like alcohol.

When a sheriff's deputy arrived at the scene, Barkman ran away, fleeing through the woods and then falling off a sixty-foot cliff in John Boyd Thacher State Park. The Albany County Sheriff's Office coordinated a rope rescue, which took two hours.

"Sheriff's deputies began yelling Erika's name and they could hear her calling for help from the bottom of the cliff, but they were unable to see her," a release from the sheriff's office says.

Once Barkman was found, she was loaded into a rescue basket and hauled up the cliff. She was taken to Albany Medical Center with non-life-threatening injuries.

## LOCAL PAGEANT WINNER DITCHES SCHOOL

A teenage beauty queen was arrested after she allegedly faked doctor's notes to skip school.

Madison Cox, Miss South Carolina Teen International 2015, was arrested after she used a pad from Parris Family Chiropractic, in Lyman, to write fake doctor's notes explaining her absences from Byrnes High School, the Duncan Police Department told reporters.

Cox was never at the clinic on the dates she used in her notes, and on some of the dates, the clinic was closed, police said.

After she was arrested, the teenager took to Twitter to express her annoyance at her new-found fame.

"Did they really just put me on the news BC I went to jail for a DOCTORS NOTE???" one Tweet read, which was later deleted. But she followed it up with, "It's sad that I'm the only entertainment in y'alls lives," complete with crying and laughing emojis.

She added, "I've got to learn to stop being so childish and keep my mouth closed."

Cox was crowned Miss South Carolina Teen International in 2015.

## LOCALS TURN TO DIY DENTISTRY

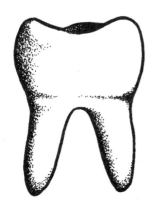

No one likes going to the dentist. But we still appreciate knowing the person we go to has a license to practice dentistry.

For two years, Elda Graciela Margez de Zamora, of Phoenix, Arizona, ran an unlicensed dental practice out of her apartment. She has now been charged with two felony counts, including fraudulent schemes and practices.

Zamora turned her apartment into a dentist's office, converting a bed into a dental chair and setting up a waiting room in her living room, complete with chairs and magazines.

Police say she also branched out into orthodontics, and even fitted her apartment manager with braces.

Some neighbors noticed that Zamora had lots of visitors, but didn't think much of it.

"There was just a lot of people going in and out, but I guessed they were friends and family," said one neighbor.

Fortunately, Zamora is not accused of physically harming her "patients," and court documents made available shortly after her arrest make no mention of the quality of her care.

## LOCAL WANTS TO STOP DOMESTIC VIOLENCE BUT CAN'T

What is the definition of irony? Perhaps it's being arrested for domestic violence while wearing a t-shirt that says, "Stop Domestic Violence."

That's what happened to Emily Wilson, from Sangerville, Maine. Wilson, a social studies teacher at Piscataquis Community High School, allegedly fired a gun and grabbed her husband during an argument in their bedroom.

Wilson believed her husband was having an affair, and in her anger, she fired a shot from a .45-caliber handgun into the mattress of the bed.

Wilson was charged with domestic violence, reckless conduct with a dangerous weapon, and domestic violence assault.

And if she doesn't already regret her actions enough, her booking photo clearly shows that she was wearing a shirt that reads "Stop Domestic Violence."

If convicted, Wilson could face five years in state prison and fines up to $5,000.

## SMUGGLERS MIGHT NOT BE GETTING SMARTER

A woman trying to enter the United States was arrested by Customs and Border Protection when her innocent-looking burritos turned out to be hiding nearly a pound of methamphetamine.

Susy Laborin was carrying a bag stuffed with what looked like delicious burritos. But when a drug-sniffing dog alerted handlers to a controlled substance, officers found the meth, according to the reports. The meth burritos were worth about $3,000.

Laborin said that she "was supposed to be paid $500 to transport the drugs via shuttle from Nogales, Arizona, to Tuscon where she would deliver them to an unknown third party."

### INEBRIATED BEAR BAIT

A man in Minot, North Dakota, snuck into a zoo after hours and was bitten by a bear.

David Shepard, and his friend Kody Nelson Kage, were under the influence of alcohol when they climbed the fence surrounding the Roosevelt Park Zoo. Shepard approached the bear enclosure and attempted to lure a bear closer to him by sticking his arm through the bars. The bear, of course, interpreted this as an invitation for a midnight snack.

Fortunately, Shepard was able to escape the jaws of the bear, and was taken to the Trinity Hospital Emergency Trauma Center, where he was treated for his injuries.

Because he was injured, police did not immediately arrest Shepard, but he was eventually charged with criminal trespassing. Considering he still has all his limbs, he got off pretty easy.

## AN UNAPPRECIATED FRIEND
## TURNS TO BURGLARY

A man in Austin, Texas, burglarized the home of a friend, and then left a confession note on the kitchen counter.

According to an affidavit, Mark Dana Kenady had visited the victim's home the night before and asked to borrow $2. The victim said he didn't have any cash on him, so Kenady left.

But the next evening, the victim returned to his apartment to discover a broken window, a flat screen television, $50 in cash, and other property were missing. The victim then saw a handwritten note in the kitchen, which was signed by Kenady. In the note, he complained about being unappreciated by the victim, and mentioned that he was still sour about being refused the $2 the night before. But he ended the note by telling the victim that he "still appreciates him."

Thanks to the note, police were able to compare the signature on the note to the signature on Kenady's driver's license, to ensure they had the right man. He was charged with burglary of a residence, a second-degree felony.

## RED LOBSTER BURNS THE ROOF OFF THE SUCKER

The roof of a Red Lobster restaurant in Grandville, Michigan, caught fire after a roofing contractor decided to take a smoke break while handling combustible materials, fire officials said.

One firefighter was hospitalized for heat exhaustion, and two roofing workers suffered minor injuries when they attempted to extinguish the flames. Firefighters were able to quickly contain the blaze, and the interior of the restaurant was undamaged.

Proving that it's never a good idea to smoke around flammable material, a fire lieutenant confirmed that the roofing contractors were using rags to clean a corner of the roof when the fire started.